JONATHAN CROALL

LETS ACT LOCALLY

THE GROWTH OF LOCAL EXCHANGE TRADING SYSTEMS

CALOUSTE GULBENKIAN FOUNDATION, LONDON

For my brother Stevie

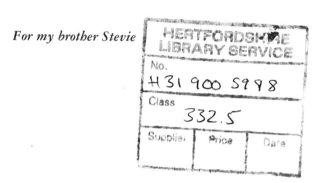
Published by the Calouste Gulbenkian Foundation
98 Portland Place
London W1N 4ET
Tel: 0171 636 5313

ISBN 0 903319 81 0

British Library Cataloguing-in-Publication Data
A catalogue record for this book is available from the British Library

Designed by Chris Hyde
Printed by Expression Printers Ltd, London N5 1JT
Distributed by Turnaround Publisher Services Ltd, Unit 3, Olympia Trading
Estate, Coburg Road, Wood Green, London N22 6TZ. Tel: 0181 829 3000

LETS ACT LOCALLY

David Simonds, *The Guardian*

By the same author

Don't Shoot the Goalkeeper (OUP)

The Parents' Day School Book (Panther)

Neill of Summerhill: The Permanent Rebel (Routledge)

All the Best, Neill: Letters from Summerhill (Deutsch)

Don't You Know There's a War On? The People's Voice 1939-1945 (Hutchinson)

Dig for History: Active Learning Across the Curriculum (Southgate)

Sent Away (OUP)

Helping to Heal: The Arts in Health Care (Calouste Gulbenkian Foundation)

Preserve or Destroy: Tourism and the Environment (Calouste Gulbenkian Foundation)

CONTENTS

ACKNOWLEDGMENTS

This book was written with the help of a great many people in different parts of the UK and Ireland. I would like to thank all those who were good enough to provide me with the information, ideas and opinions which form its core.

Unfortunately there is not space here to mention them all by name. But I would like to single out those who gave me invaluable help with the case-studies, and to thank them for being so generous with their time and hospitality: Anne O'Carroll in Beara, County Cork; Mal and Jenny Neumann in Banbridge, County Down; John Rogers and Tony Care in South Powys; Patrick Boase in Glasgow; Rose Snow, Felicity Glass and Siobhan Harpur in Manchester; Sally Moxon and Simon Raven in Suffolk; Jenny Banfield in Stroud; and David Williams and Sue Shaw in Hounslow. I would also like to thank Liz Shephard for her invaluable help in putting me in touch with many LETS groups in England and Wales, and Lesley Rowan and Mal Neumann for doing the same for Scotland and Northern Ireland.

Thanks also to Colin Ward, who as always drew my attention to a number of very useful sources of information and ideas. Finally, I would like to thank the Director of the Gulbenkian Foundation, Ben Whitaker, for commissioning me to write a book on this intriguing subject.

INTRODUCTION

'Power is never given away by the powerful, it has to be taken by the weak' – Richard Douthwaite, *Short Circuit*

The global market economy has arrived with a vengeance. As it tightens its grip on communities around the world, so the way we live is becoming increasingly dominated by the decisions of the multinational companies and by the international banks and financiers who control the supply of money.

The pressure on individual enterprise is growing. In the UK the number of small shops has halved in the last 30 years; by the year 2000 it is estimated that almost half of what we spend our money on will be provided by just 250 companies. It is estimated that 0.1% of the population owns 50% of the sterling wealth. Meanwhile the World Bank reports that 95% of global money circulation is speculative, with less than 5% related to real commodity trade.

These trends are having a devastating effect on many communities, where money is in short supply, small businesses are collapsing at an alarming rate, and high rates of unemployment have become a permanent feature of many people's lives. This in turn has led to a breakdown of community values and an increase in social isolation, especially but by no means exclusively among poorer sections of society.

In recent years many local initiatives have been launched in an attempt to counter these trends, including community businesses, credit unions, self-build schemes, and other projects. In some areas these have made a real impact, giving people a greater measure of control over their lives, and helping to revitalise rundown or fragmented communities.

One idea that has recently caught many people's imagination is the Local Exchange Trading System, popularly known as LETS. There are now over 400 LETS groups in the UK, and a further 30 established in Ireland. The basic principles are beautifully simple but potentially subversive: that people don't need money in order to buy and sell goods and services, that they can create their own currency and their own wealth, and in doing so help both to improve their local economy and enhance the social networks in their community.

The growing popularity of LETS during the 1990s has attracted a great deal of attention from the media. An increasing number of researchers are finding the subject fertile ground for academic study. Influential books such as Guy Dauncey's *After the Crash* and Richard Douthwaite's *Short Circuit* have deepened many people's understanding of where the idea fits into the wider framework of community regeneration, while Peter Lang's *LETS Work* has provided a valuable handbook on the practicalities of setting up and running a LETS.

This book provides a picture of the LETS landscape as it was in the spring of 1997. Based on visits to a small cross-section of LETS groups around the UK and Ireland, and contacts with people in dozens of others, it tries to get beyond the slogans, the theories and the research questionnaires to look at how LETS actually operate in the real world. It reports on the real benefits that people have gained from their involvement in LETS groups, but also examines the many problems they have encountered along the way, including legal ones. It examines some of the interesting recent developments linking LETS to food, housing, mental health and education, and the growing involvement of local authorities and small businesses. Finally, it suggests some of the issues that need to be tackled if the LETS idea is to continue to grow and develop in the twenty-first century.

HISTORY

1. HISTORY

'If labour be the parent of wealth, why were workers of the country compelled to starve when they were able and anxious to work?' – Robert Owen, social reformer

L ETS is essentially an old idea in new clothing. It has close links with the traditional notion of barter, which has been used as a method of exchanging goods ever since communities have existed. But barter has obvious limitations, since it involves reciprocal trading between two parties who may not be able to match each other's needs. This was one of the reasons for the gradual appearance of tokens, whose trading value could be agreed for a basic range of goods and services.

In many communities in times past the token of exchange was not initially a coin, but common objects such as grain, bricks, furs, axes, swords, mats, shells, hides or feathers. In the seventeenth century playing cards were marked to pay the royal troops in Canada during a coin shortage. Later, in the states of Virginia, Maryland and Carolina in America, receipts for the staple crop of tobacco were used as tokens of exchange for more than 150 years.

One notable experiment in Britain was the National Equitable Labour Exchange, set up in 1832 by the radical social reformer and visionary Robert Owen to help unemployed people meet each other's needs. The exchange printed its own currency in the form of Labour Notes, expressed in terms of hours. While it was briefly successful, its failure was due in part to the fact that it was unable to supply such workers with the commodity they needed most, which was food.[1]

The idea that the state should have a monopoly on the right to mint coins and print paper money is a comparatively recent one. In the UK it was the Bank Charter Act of 1844 that gave this right to the state. Until then, local currencies had been the norm. Often during the Industrial Revolution the coin of the realm ran short, and local banks issued notes for circulation within their area. Meanwhile some large employers paid their workers in their own printed currency or token coinage, which was accepted not only within their home town but also outside.[2]

Local currencies flourished again in Europe and the USA during the Depression of the 1930s. One of the most successful was that used in Wörgl in Austria, where the town's tax and employment crisis was solved and poverty changed to prosperity in just one year by the creation of a local currency. Some 200 other communities in Austria announced their intention of following suit, until the Central Bank, fearing it would lose control over the money supply, threatened the Wörgl council with legal proceedings, and brought the experiment to an end. A similar venture in Bavaria also ran foul of the central banking authorities.[3]

A more enduring experiment began in 1815 in Guernsey, at a time when the Channel Island had been badly affected by the Napoleonic Wars. Its creation of interest-free notes enabled buildings and dykes to be repaired, and brought prosperity to a previously depressed economy. Private banks that arrived on the island tried unsuccessfully to squeeze the local currency out of existence. Today it still exists alongside sterling.[4]

The mutual aid element of LETS also has plenty of historical antecedents, notably in those working-class communities where people built up their sick clubs, coffin clubs, penny banks and building societies. Such communities were commonplace in the Britain of the 1930s, and were a considerable factor in helping families to survive in a time of high unemployment.

In Ireland mutual aid within and between small farming communities was based on the *meitheal*, a system of favours done between neighbours that is only now dying out.[5]

In the 1970s there was a revival of interest in LETS-style schemes and mutual aid networks. One of the most successful of these was Link, a scheme started in 1975. Initially designed to help elderly people living in urban areas to keep mentally and physically fit and develop new contacts, it encouraged them to do small tasks for other members of the scheme, and to be paid in stamps based on a system representing an exchange of time.

Link later broadened to include people of all ages, and at one time had a network of 35 groups in operation. It was not, however, a self-supporting or sustainable scheme, since it was dependent on financial and other kinds of support from charities such as Age Concern.[6]

The idea of LETS, then, has a number of antecedents, many of which flourished at a time of economic depression or recession. It is perhaps significant that LETS were born and grew up in the economically difficult years of the 1980s and early 1990s.

PIONEERS
AND
PRINCIPLES

2. PIONEERS AND PRINCIPLES

'To say that people cannot exchange value with one another because there is no money is like saying you cannot build a house because you have no feet and inches' – Allan Watts, philosopher

L ETS groups have been set up for a variety of reasons, none of them mutually exclusive. Among those most often mentioned by founding members are:

- to regenerate the local economy;
- to enable people to have more control over the goods and services they obtain;
- to make their exchange a more personal transaction;
- to develop a greater community spirit;
- to improve social contacts and lessen social isolation;
- to enable people to use skills that might otherwise be wasted;
- to bolster the confidence and self-esteem of people not in paid work;
- to have a good time and improve the quality of life.

Although LETS have taken a number of forms in different countries, the basic model for the systems now being developed in the UK and Ireland was set up by a community activist in Canada in the early 1980s. Michael Linton lived in the small mining community of Courtenay on Vancouver Island, where unemployment was at a high level because of the recent closure of the local mine. After he and others had tried unsuccessfully to use barter as a means of gaining their livelihood, he devised a system which put barter onto a non-profit-making, community-wide basis, using a specially created currency known as the 'green dollar'. Originally labelled a Local Employment and Trade System, Courtenay LETS started trading in 1983. After two years it had 500 members, and a trading record that was the equivalent of $300,000. The scheme received a great deal of publicity nationally and the idea started to spread through Canada. Today there are about a dozen LETS up and running.

LETS has also taken off in a big way in Australia, where there are now more than 200 groups, almost a quarter of them in Western Australia. The first to start trading, in 1987, was in a small 'alternative' community in Maleny, Queensland, the home town of a permaculture specialist, Jill Jordan, who was inspired by Michael Linton's ideas. Other groups soon sprang up. The largest group in the world, in the Blue Mountains area west of Sydney, began in

1991, and by spring 1997 had gathered 2,000 members. New Zealand too became interested in the idea, and by 1995 had 50 groups actively trading.

In the United States, the idea has developed in a number of different ways, with the emphasis on various types of community currency. One of the most successful schemes is that started by a former journalist and publisher Paul Glover in Ithaca, New York, where members of the community use their own 'Ithaca Hours' paper currency. Since 1991 some 2,000 people have been involved, and have traded to the tune of an estimated $2 million. Similar 'Hours' systems are being developed in 18 other US cities. Another variation is the Time Dollar, started by lawyer Edgar Cahn in Washington. This scheme enables older members of a community to offer services to others, and to build up credit against the time when they might need such services themselves. Time Dollar systems are now in operation in 38 states in the US.

More recently the idea has caught on in Europe. There are now 124 systems operating in France, 100 in Italy, 65 in the Netherlands, and many in Spain, Germany, Switzerland, Denmark and other countries. The idea has proved popular in Japan, and is beginning to be explored in the former East Germany and other parts of the former Soviet bloc in Eastern Europe. But the fastest growth recently has been in the UK and the Republic of Ireland.

From tentative beginnings, LETS have now firmly taken root. By 1992 there were 35 systems in operation in the UK, by 1993 more than 100, and by 1994 the figure had reached 200. In 1997 there are over 400 groups, involving 35,000 people. Around 35 of these groups are in Scotland, 20 in Wales and three in Northern Ireland. A further 30 are up and running in Ireland.

The idea of LETS was introduced to the UK in 1985, at The Other Economic Summit, a forum for 'new economics' thinkers run by the New Economic Foundation, which was an early active promoter of the LETS idea. The NEF raised money for a tour by Michael Linton, who talked about his experience in Canada. The first LETS group was established the same year, in Norwich. Growth was initially slow: three years later there were still only a handful of groups, mainly in the West Country.

The early LETS groups in the UK and Ireland tended to be set up in small towns or rural areas, within a well-defined and predominantly middle-class community. Usually the moving force was a small band of enthusiasts, with

15

one individual often acting as the catalyst. Many of these groups were started by people active in environmental politics, the green movement or the Green Party. This was certainly the case in Norwich and in West Wiltshire. Others, notably in Stroud and Totnes, were already involved in an 'alternative' lifestyle, and were therefore perhaps more receptive to an idea such as LETS that stood outside the mainstream economy.

But as the idea spread to the larger towns and cities, the social composition of LETS began to broaden, and the proportion of unemployed members to increase. Gradually, as the recession bit deeper in the early 1990s, groups began to spring up in inner-city areas and on large estates, where there were often high levels of unemployment. While it was often community development workers and other professionals who started the ball rolling in these areas, people on low or no incomes slowly started to participate.

Two events led to a dramatic increase in interest. The first was the publication in 1988 of Guy Dauncey's influential book *After the Crash: The Emergence of the Rainbow Economy*, which introduced many people to the idea of LETS for the first time. The second was the setting up in 1990 of LetsLink UK, a national body providing advice, guidelines, resources and an umbrella organisation for the growing number of independent local groups, as well as a central point of contact for the increasingly interested media. Subsequently other bodies were established, such as LETS Solutions and LETSGo, which aimed to broaden and widen the concept and practice of LETS, and which adopted an approach substantially different from the one favoured by LetsLink.

Several councils are now offering support to groups as part of their anti-poverty or community development strategies, or as a result of projects initiated under the banner of Local Agenda 21. One of the outcomes of the 1992 Rio Earth Summit, this invites local communities to produce their own visions for a more sustainable lifestyle, looking at such questions as ethical shopping, food and agriculture, economy and work, and others that overlap both practically and philosophically with LETS.

Like credit unions and community businesses, housing and food co-operatives, and other self-help schemes, LETS are increasingly being looked at for their potential for community development and for regenerating local economies. How then do these systems actually operate on the ground?

CASE STUDY
SMALL TOWN: STROUD

One of Stroud's more offbeat shops, in a place that has its fair share of them, stands at the top of the steep and narrow high street of this small but lively Gloucestershire town. It stocks a colourful variety of pure cotton clothes, made in India and sold directly to this workers' co-operative. Run by the Bishopston Trading Company as part of a charitable Third World project, its aim is to enable the weavers and tailors who produce the goods to obtain a decent wage and a range of healthcare and other benefits.

But this 'fair trading' element is not the only unconventional feature of the shop. On one wall hangs a LETS noticeboard, covered with cards and leaflets offering circle dancing, puppetry, guitar lessons, reflexology, and much more besides. This small business is just one of around a dozen in Stroud where you can buy goods or services with a mixture of sterling and the local currency, strouds. Others include a wholefood café, a land care service, a cycle firm, and a natural health clinic.

Jane Brown, the Bishopston shop's manager, sees several advantages in belonging to a LETS:

> 'Many of our customers are mums who would normally go to Oxfam or jumble sales for clothes. They come here partly because of the fair trading, but also because they know that, if they're paying 25% of the price in strouds, they can afford to buy something a bit better, as a treat for themselves or their children. So now quite a lot of our regulars use the LETS currency, which also means extra business for the shop, since people using strouds tend to buy more anyway.'

Her main problem has been to spend the strouds the shop has accumulated – at present its account is in credit to the tune of 600, so the spring sale has had to be a 'sterling only' one. But ways have been found round this obstacle. One woman who does sewing and alterations to the clothes from home has accepted 100% of her wages in the currency, and two part-time staff have sometimes accepted part of theirs in this form. The labour involved in building a new shop front has also been covered by strouds, as has payment for the printing of the company's mail-order catalogue.

Stroud LETS, established in 1990, was one of the first in the UK. For some of the pioneers it seemed like an ideal place in which to start a system. A town of 15,000 people, it has a long tradition of radical politics and artistic activity, and was the first council in the UK to be run by the Green Party. Like Totnes and Glastonbury, it has become a magnet for many of those attracted to an alternative lifestyle. The town and its surrounding valleys are bristling with the self-employed, offering everything from tree care to craniosacral therapy, from environmental home audits to desktop publishing. If a novel idea such as LETS couldn't get off the ground here, the thinking went, what chance would it stand in more conservatively minded areas?

Today the system is well-grounded in the everyday life of the community. It embraces both Stroud itself and its surrounding villages (including Slad, made famous by Laurie Lee in *Cider with Rosie*). It has an office in town manned by a rota of part-time administrators, with a new computer system set up with the help of a £1,000 grant from the council. During the last two months of 1996 the system recorded 930 transactions, resulting in a turnover of 13,800 strouds. After reaching a plateau a little while back, membership has started to increase again, and by spring 1997 there were 320 active members.

One member who was initially very sceptical of the system was Roger Berry, a mental health commissioner and forestry worker. 'I was extremely suspicious, I saw it as another piece of Stroud whimsy, to go with the nut cutlets and the open-toed sandals,' he recalls. He was eventually persuaded by the system's administrator to list all the skills he had to offer, which were then printed in the LETS directory. To his surprise his services – for laying hedges, killing and plucking chickens, and breaking into houses when people locked themselves out – were soon much in demand.

The group's membership is mainly middle-class, including professionals such as accountants and solicitors, as well as older retired people. 'Although there's quite a big alternative scene here, the LETS is not just for ageing hippies – though I confess to being one myself,' says Maggie Mills, one of the founding members. 'But I suppose there is quite a big division between the local folk and the incomers – though some of us have been here for 25 or 30 years, and are active in small businesses and local politics.'

Currently the town's mayor, she also owns and runs Mills Café, an attractive wholefood eating place just off the high street, which she enrolled in the system from the beginning. Like the Bishopston shop it is well in credit in strouds at present, so LETS trading is confined to payment for food, and in the evenings only. To spend the café's strouds, Maggie Mills encourages LETS members to bring in vegetables in large quantities from their gardens for her to buy. She has also paid for plumbing and wiring services in strouds.

Other businesses in the town have come and gone within the system. At one time a firm of solicitors belonged, feeling that this brought in custom from people who would not normally use a solicitor. The present membership includes the local Rudolf Steiner School, which takes 10% of parents' fees in strouds 'by agreement'. Two local food traders also belong. Twice a week a market is held in Stroud in the Shambles, an attractive space next to the old Cotswold stone town hall. Here organic vegetables can be bought for 20% strouds, while curry, dhal, samosas, rice and other Indian food can be ordered in bulk for anything up to 100%. Girish Patel, who runs the latter stall, says: 'I like the idea of keeping things local, and this is a good way of making contact with people.'

Attracting local businesses into the system has been just one of the challenges. Those involved in running the system in Stroud have at some time had to face most of the problems thrown up by the LETS concept. One such is the question of whether or not to set limits to people's trading – in which large 'positive' balances can be as much of a problem as substantial 'negative' ones. According to one member, people have been known to be 1,000 strouds in debit. Up to now no limits have been formally set, in part because no one is sure what sum would be appropriate. Meanwhile the administrators keep a regular check on people's accounts, and if any large balances are uncovered they are published in the newsletter.

The rate for the job has also been a tricky issue to resolve. In Stroud the agreed philosophy is that the rate, and the proportion for which payment in strouds is acceptable, should normally be negotiable between the two parties concerned. Only where this is not the case will the rate be stated in the directory. But people's behaviour is not always predictable or controllable. Jenny Banfield, who joined the system in 1993, describes a typical progression. 'People start on the bottom floor, perhaps needing to raise their self-esteem,' she says. 'Then they get very busy, so they move on to trading on a 50% strouds, 50% sterling basis. Then they get even better known, and decide they can't afford to work with the local currency any more.'

Some LETS members feel that this attitude could easily undermine the whole system. Andy Read, who always charges 100% in strouds for his own services (pet sitting, gardening, press publicity, bar-work), recently found that four people he phoned about their services would trade for no more than five to 20% in strouds.

> 'It has to stop, things are getting out of hand. I appreciate some services require expenditure of real pounds, and that it's fully justified to recoup these. However, all my examples were for services which required no more than people's time and effort. Surely in these cases anything less than 50% strouds is taking the mickey out of the system and its members? It acts as a huge deterrent to trading. Furthermore, I'm now starting to come across members who previously accepted a high proportion of strouds, but who have had to drop their percentage because they find them so hard to spend.'

In his view such people are going against the spirit of the system, and should be asked to leave it.

Much of course depends on the reasons people have for joining the scheme, and in what way they are prepared to balance the economic and mutual aid elements of trading. Helena Petre, a part-time publisher's researcher, moved to Stroud partly in order to join the LETS. She offers tuition in English as a foreign language and aromatherapy massage, and usually accepts 33% for the latter. 'But if a client is very badly off, I will do it for 100%,' she says. 'I see LETS as being a useful support network.' John Rhodes, a long-standing member who does tree surgery and landscaping, also believes in adapting his rates according to the customer, and will sometimes go up to 95% in strouds for people in financial difficulties. 'What the hell, I don't need lots of money, and it's a nice way of doing business,' he observes.

While Stroud is clearly a LETS success story, there is a down side. With a steady growth in membership in its seven-year life, and new members still joining, the system has reached a level where people no longer know most of their fellow traders. Inevitably, it now has a rather less personal feel to it. 'People tend to let others do the work, and then moan about the system,' Maggie Mills admits. 'There used to be rather more of a feeling that it was everybody's scheme.'

NUTS AND BOLTS

3

3. NUTS AND BOLTS

'LETS is a brilliant idea: the problem is translating it in to practice' – member of Camden LETS

T he diversity of shape, size and style within the LETS network is one of the strengths of the idea. Where a hundred flowers are allowed to bloom, systems can adapt to local circumstances and needs. But while every LETS is different from the next one – if only because the people running and belonging to it are different – most have certain organisational features in common.

Getting started

Many groups have started as a result of one or two individuals taking the initiative, perhaps after reading a newspaper article about LETS, or hearing about it from someone already involved in a group. Others are formed by a small group of like-minded people who for one reason or another see a need for a system in their community. A handful of more recent groups have been started as a result of prompting from community activists, or by LETS development workers employed by the local council.

Once established a system is usually run by a committee or core group, typically consisting of around half a dozen people. Normally they will divide up between them the essential tasks: handling the accounts, compiling and updating the directory, dealing with membership inquiries, looking after publicity, organising trading and social activities. If the group has an office, it is normally run by a rota of volunteers.

Members of a LETS create their own local unit of exchange, and give it a name. The unit may be exactly equal in value to the national currency unit; or be linked to it, but 'floating' in value; or related in some way to an hour's work.

Each person in a system compiles a list of the goods and services they might want, and those they feel they can offer. This information is then put into a directory, which is circulated to all members of the group, and updated regularly as new members join. Some groups charge a joining or annual membership fee, which is credited to the system's own account; others go to the opposite extreme and offer new members a modest number of units to open their account, to encourage them to trade.

When people start to trade with each other, they may do so on the basis of an agreed rate, price or number of hours. Alternatively the rates may be negotiable between the two parties involved in any transaction. Once the transaction is complete, the 'buyer' generally gives the 'seller' a 'cheque' for the agreed amount, and this is recorded by a central administrator. Accounts are often regularly circulated to all members of the group.

'Wants' and 'offers'

The 'wants' and 'offers' of LETS members inevitably vary from group to group. In predominately middle-class areas the list of goods and services on offer tends to be top-heavy with alternative therapies. Wellington LETS in Somerset, for example, offers acupuncture, counselling, foot massage, movement therapy, reflexology, yoga, stress relief, and polarity therapy, among others. Arts and crafts also tend to feature heavily in such groups: in King's Lynn and West Norfolk LETS punch-needle embroidery, tie-dying, bead jewellery-making, candle-making, leatherwork and dried-flower arranging are just a few of more than 50 services on offer. Many such schemes have a range of produce available, such as the organic vegetables, homemade bread, goat's milk and special desserts listed in the Carlisle LETS directory.

Other schemes manage to cater for people's more mundane but essential needs. Brighton LETS is hot on repairs and maintenance (of cars, bikes, carpets, clothes, videos and much else) and building and construction (carpentry, joinery, furniture-making, roofing). Derby has an extensive gardening section, in which members offer plant care, lawn mowing, compost, shrub removal, design advice, and assistance with dry-stone walling. In Ealing LETS you can choose from carpet shampooing, washing and ironing, rubbish removal, shopping, dog walking, cat grooming and pet sitting. And members of the West Wiltshire group have access to the most basic service of all, with a midwife offering her services in local currency.

In most directories the offers tend to outnumber the wants, sometimes spectacularly. A few groups, such as Haverfordwest and Lancaster, list only offers, in the belief that to include 'wants' is unnecessary. Instead they encourage members to supply information about individual 'wants' for the regular newsletter.

Local currencies

The chance to create their own currency has prompted groups to come up with a wide variety of names. Many of these have a monetary flavour, either ancient or modern, as with the talents used in North Devon and the Gipping Valley in Suffolk, the groats to be found in Stirling and West Glasgow, the pledges favoured by North London, and the readies used for trading in Tralee in County Kerry and, inevitably, in Reading. Other groups have opted for a name drawn from their native language. Thus in Galway they trade with the *luach* (meaning 'worth' or 'value'); in Nithsdale, Dumfries and Galloway, they use the *doonie* (short for the Scots word *doonhamer*, meaning 'down homer'); while in the Vale of Clwyd the unit is the *ddraig* (dragon).

Local geographical references abound, often in the form of rivers – as in Southampton's solents, Castle in Shropshire's onnys, Lancaster's lunes, Tweed's tweeds, Exeter's exes. Other landmarks also feature, as in the case of Sligo's gills, Barnes' ponds, Westport in County Mayo's reeks, and South Powys' and Malvern's beacons. Some currencies reflect the industrial history of the area, as with Manchester's bobbins (cotton), Newcastle's nuts (shipbuilding), North-East Dartmoor's tins (mining) or Thameside's anchors (dockyards). Others suggest an interest in a more romantic or mystic past: Carlisle uses reivers in honour of the celebrated border raiders, while Avalon in Glastonbury uses the *gebo*, a runic symbol. In the Moray Firth they have opted for a real local myth, and chosen nessies.

Several groups have kept a straight face in choosing their name. So Stroud has strouds, Newbury new berries, Stoke stokers, Bradford brads, and Bute butes. Others have risked a jokier label: in Hackney they use favours, in Donegal they've gone for sods, in Cleveland they get by on doofers, in Belfast they actually trade in pints, and in Derby, seemingly at a loss to make up their minds, they have opted for wadevas.

Membership

Although some LETS remain merely groups of individuals, an increasing number are drawing in groups and organisations. Many have attempted to involve businesses, though with only limited success. (See chapter 6.) In some areas – for instance Hounslow and Suffolk – voluntary organisations have been persuaded to sign up, while in Frome, Calderdale and elsewhere the local council has joined. Other bodies that have got involved include schools and colleges, sports clubs, charities, disabled groups, mental health service users, Women's Institutes, music groups, performing venues, arts societies, and village and church halls.

In a few areas special efforts have been made to involve older people in the idea. In one area in England the University of the Third Age was the catalyst; in Stranraer in Scotland it was the Pensioner Power organisation. However, neither really got off the ground, the latter because there was already a strong, informal network of support in the neighbourhood.

Children have been welcomed in many groups: Falmouth has several 12 and 13 year-olds; Newcastle's youngest member is 10; and Manchester has had an eight year-old member, offering card tricks for a bobbin. In South Shropshire they have a special section in the directory for children, where offers of lawn mowing, raking up leaves and hiring out computer games are listed. In Salisbury they even have a separate group known as KETS – Kids Exchange and Trading Scheme – which trades in kebbles (while the adults trade in ebbles). Safeguards in groups where children under 16 are involved tend to be along the lines of those in South Somerset, whereby children can only trade with their parent's or guardian's permission, and need their written approval for any offers or wants they decide to submit to the directory.

Trading

The majority of trading transactions take place in people's homes. But most groups also hold some kind of regular gathering or social event, at which people can get to know their fellow-members and make new contacts for trading. This may take the form of an auction, a fair, a 'joining party', a sale of goods, a family day, a barbecue, a musical performance, or simply an

25

evening in the pub. Some groups, such as Stowmarket and Stonham in Suffolk, hold 'themed' trading evenings, designed to encourage trading in a particular category of services.

Rates of exchange

A recent survey of LETS revealed that only a small minority (13%) fix their local currency unit to sterling: the rest either have a unit related to the pound but 'floating' against it (79%), or have some other arrangement, usually based on a time system (13%). This is in marked contrast to an earlier survey, which showed two-thirds of LETS groups linking their unit of exchange to the pound, and one-third setting a different value.[1]

Many groups go for the 'floating' option for ideological reasons, believing that the less their system is linked to the mainstream economy, with its attendant interest rates, inflation, scarcity, and devaluation, the better. Most leave individuals to negotiate a rate for the job between themselves, though many recommend a rate for guidance. In North-East Dartmoor the guideline banding is seven to 12 tins an hour; in Lewes the recommended rate is 12 trugs to the hour; in Falmouth it is five palms an hour, the palm being loosely linked to the pound sterling.

Reducing inequalities

Some groups base their rates on a desire to narrow the gap between traditionally highly-paid professional services and lower-paid activities such as cleaning or gardening. In Brighton, for example, trading is based on an average rate of 12 brights an hour, whatever the transaction may be. A similar system works in Lancaster, where the standard rate is 10 lunes. 'Most members stick to this guideline,' says co-ordinator Sue Cowgill. 'Linking the currency to sterling is something we've always avoided, in order to level out some of the inequalities in how different jobs are valued.'

But sometimes the idea can divide a group. Nick Hope Wilson, co-ordinator of South Somerset LETS, admits:

'We've had a degree of aggro and a very heated debate about pricing.

Some people felt strongly that everyone's time was of equal value, while others felt, equally strongly, that professional skills were of greater worth than, say, babysitting or dog walking. We solved this by agreeing that we didn't want unnecessary rules, and that we weren't in a LETS to be told what to do. So we fixed a recommended rate, and left it up to the individuals concerned to negotiate.'

To encourage flexibility and the maximum participation, payment for services may sometimes be made partly in national currency and partly in local. This is most likely to happen where businesses are involved, to allow for the cost of raw materials or overheads.

Setting limits

This is particularly useful where there are anxieties about people trading too much or too little. People who seem reluctant to trade, for instance, can then be specifically targeted by other members taking up their 'offers'. Where this happens, groups have used different approaches. In some the administrator will contact the member informally, and find out if there's a problem. In others limits will be set: North-East Dartmoor LETS, for instance, recently set a credit limit of 500 tins. Another method is to give new members a set of cheques with a low value, and only allow them to apply for ones of a greater value once they have a track record in trading.

Accountability

A LETS is essentially based on trust, and could not work successfully without this ingredient. This is why transparency is often considered crucial. Most groups consider it worthwhile to have a set of model rules, usually called a members' agreement, while many have put the system on an even more formal basis by adopting a constitution. A members' agreement covers matters such as the status and aims of the LETS, details of its organisation, and the rights and obligations of the members. It also ensures that the group is properly covered for liability, data protection, and so on.

One rule which many see as important is the right of any member to have access to the details of the trading balance and turnover of other members. Many groups make a point of publishing these in their newsletter from time to time. The accounts will also show whether any individual has built up a large imbalance, and the group has then to decide when and if to take any action.

If a member leaves the system while seriously in debit – in practice this very rarely happens – the amount is normally divided among the membership, or just written off. Another way of coping with this situation is to have a special 'leavers' account', to which any members who leave can donate their credits. These can then be used to cover any debt left by a leaver.

Inter-trading

Many systems confine their activities to their own membership. But as their numbers have grown, so the idea of 'inter-trading' or setting up a 'Multi-LETS' with one or more neighbouring LETS has started to develop.

Inter-trading requires convertibility between local currencies, or the creation of a new one. It is now widespread in several areas, especially, though not exclusively, rural ones. In Norfolk the eight LETS groups have recently introduced the practice, as have the 12 in neighbouring Suffolk. Devon, the county with the largest number of LETS (18), and Cornwall (9) have held county-wide meetings and area LETS forums, although inter-trading between individual systems has only just started. There have also been examples of inter-trading in cities such as Bristol, London and Manchester.

The idea of a multi-LETS system is to cover a larger area than that of a single LETS, with all the accounts of the individual system centralised under one 'registry'. Once a person joins a registry, they can open accounts with any system within the multi-LETS, thereby gaining access to a much wider range of goods and services.

These then are the basic features of a LETS. The next two chapters look at the many benefits which groups and individuals have gained from the systems, and at the principal problems which they have encountered.

CASE STUDY
OUTER LONDON BOROUGH
HOUNSLOW

The position could hardly be more central. Walk down the busy Cranford High Street in the London Borough of Hounslow and you come to St Christopher's Church Hall. A few yards further on you find the Margaret Axhorn Medical Centre, the base for the drop-in centre run by the Cranford Good Neighbours Scheme.

These two venues have been at the heart of the operation of Hounslow LETS since its launch in autumn 1994. The church hall, one of two in the borough to belong to the system, has been frequently used for LETS activities, with the hiring charge being paid in cranes, the local currency unit. And the medical centre is where Sue Shaw, co-ordinator of the Cranford Good Neighbours Scheme, has been masterminding the development of the system since its beginnings.

Hounslow is an Outer London borough of some 200,000 residents. Cranford is a mixed area, not untypical of many in such boroughs, where poverty, unemployment and poor accommodation exist in close proximity to relative prosperity and affluence. Locally the A4 Bath Road is dubbed the 'Berlin Wall': on one side live the owner-occupiers, many with two cars to their name; on the other people in rented accommodation, much of it blighted by the noise of aircraft landing at nearby Heathrow Airport. Here live many refugees and immigrants – Asian, Somali, Algerian – in some cases three families to a house.

Sue Shaw outlines the difficulties:

> 'We work with a lot of people with real cash-flow problems. Language is also a problem: some of the refugees have university degrees but no English. But trading is less in middle-class skills; people use it more for practical things like getting lifts to the shops, or for plumbing. That makes sense when the call-out charge for a plumber can be as much as £35.'

The Hounslow LETS directory of wants and offers seems to reflect this bias: listed alongside the obligatory hypnotherapy, tarot reading and vegetarian cooking are services such as window repairing, welfare benefits help, debt counselling, ironing, respite help for carers, assistance with CVs, wills advice, and clothes alteration. The multi-ethnic nature of the membership is also evident in the appearance of Asian, Spanish and Creole cooking, and tuition in Greek, Hindi and Farsi conversation.

There are the usual problems in getting people to trade, exacerbated by the low income of many LETS members. 'People have a very cash-based mindset, it's very difficult to get them to accept that this isn't money,' Sue Shaw says. 'I try to explain that it doesn't matter, that you should just trade, because if you've spent some cranes, then someone else has got them.' She feels the geography of the borough doesn't help: stretching from Chiswick to Feltham, it makes accessibility difficult for some, especially those without a car. 'People are loathe to spend money even on bus fares, so they tend to trade only in their own immediate area.'

As elsewhere, there is also some mistrust of the system, reflecting an anxiety about the possibility of losing benefits. 'I spend a lot of time telling people not to worry, but there is a concern that if they trade too much people will start to ask questions,' Sue Shaw observes. Disability Benefit presents a particular problem. 'If a disabled person is seen to do gardening within the system, does that make them fit enough to work?'

Although her original remit as a community worker was to set up a LETS in Cranford, she was reluctant also to become its treasurer and administrator. Happily she was able at that moment to team up with Hounslow's new LETS development worker, for whom the Cranford group was to prove a useful blueprint.

Appointed in 1994 as part of the borough's anti-poverty strategy, David Williams was the first person to work on LETS full time for a local authority. He points out the advantages:

> 'You need a champion, someone to sing the idea from the rooftops, and I was dead keen. Working full time meant that I could fast-track things that take others a long time, and get access to services such as the council's internal mail. I could advertise and promote the scheme, but the impetus had to come from the people themselves.'

His initial mailing to hundreds of local people and voluntary groups was not very productive. It was only when he took a stall in a shopping mall in the middle of the borough, talked to people face to face about the idea, and invited them individually to a public meeting, that he began to get a good response from a broad cross-section. 'Personal contact was much more effective than letters or posters,' he remembers.

At the meeting, to which some 50 people came, he first asked them to write down the things they liked to do and those they hated to do. After breaking them into small groups so they could find out what other people had listed, he then got them to write down their offers. These immediately provided the basis for the first Hounslow LETS directory.

One potential barrier to convincing people that a LETS is a serious venture can be the name of the local currency. In Hounslow it was originally suggested it should be turpin, since one of the places where the notorious highwayman was known to have held up travellers was Hounslow Heath. But this was eventually felt to be too negative a label, and people opted instead for crane, after the local river. David Williams says:

'The trouble with these odd or funny names is that they can be a real block to people's understanding of what a LETS is about. People stop listening to what you're saying while they wonder what the hell a crane is. It leads them to ridicule the idea, and the whole discussion becomes a joke.'

Another difficulty, though not one unique to Hounslow, has been to persuade people joining the system to be realistic about their offers. David Williams suggests:

'Some people tend to over-sell themselves, and then let people down when they realise they can't actually find the time. My advice when it comes to the directory is not to list what you're good at, but what you can realistically do. After all it's not an ego trip.'

The Hounslow group charges an enrolment fee of £3 and five cranes, the latter being used to cover work done on the directory and the accounts. Members use a conventional home-made cheque book in their transactions, and trade at a recommended rate of six cranes an hour. However some of those who have joined live on estates, don't have a bank account, and are not used to using a cheque book. To encourage them to trade, vouchers have now been introduced into the system, based on 10 minutes of 'standard' time. The administrator sits the member down and gets them to write out a crane cheque for a certain amount of vouchers, which is then debited to the system's account. As David Williams explains:

'In this way people can trade as they always have, treating the vouchers as money. Normally of course every transaction is recorded centrally, but with this method you have to estimate, because you don't know exactly how many of the vouchers are in circulation.'

Although no special effort has been made to recruit businesses, some half a dozen have joined, mostly sole traders. Ten voluntary groups have also joined, including a luncheon club, a post-natal group, a women's support group, and a community project. And at one stage the council's own housing department was a member and traded with the LETS administration.

Like other established groups, Hounslow LETS is now experiencing a low, with little trading taking place. But there are hopes that the offer of new office facilities and a computer in Brentford will provide a new lease of life, and enable the core group to tap in to the interest and enthusiasm for LETS that they see around them.

THE
BENEFITS

4

4. THE BENEFITS

'The system encourages trust and friendship, not suspicion, and this quality seems to permeate the transactions that occur within it' – Guy Dauncey, *After the Crash*

L ETS have the potential to provide a whole range of benefits for both individuals and communities. During their relatively short existence in the UK and Ireland they have had a significant impact on many people's lives, and played a part in improving the spirit and enhancing the identity of particular communities.

At a personal level, the benefits of LETS have been many and varied. They have allowed people in all walks of life to use neglected, undervalued or new skills; given them access to goods and services which they might not normally be able to afford; helped them to improve their personal confidence and self-esteem; and, by combating social isolation, widened their social contacts and network of friends.

Unemployed people

LETS have perhaps been of most value to unemployed people. It has been estimated that on average around a quarter of those involved in LETS groups are unemployed. Some groups have a significantly higher rate: in Manchester it has been 43%, in Kingston, Surrey 50%, in Haverfordwest in Pembrokeshire as much as 70%.

In general, the membership of those LETS formed since 1994 tends to have a broader base, and therefore a higher proportion of unemployed people, than that of longer-established groups. LETS has helped many to keep in touch with the labour market, often providing them with a stepping-stone into paid work, and sometimes even the opportunity to set up their own business.

For people living in such circumstances, or those on very low incomes, the chance to trade can open up many horizons. Since trading is interest-free, it means they can obtain many essential goods and services without the need for any capital outlay. At the same time they are able to get back into the field of work, even if it is not paid employment.

Cathy Morris is a mother of two children who was unemployed for 15 years. By joining Manchester LETS she was able to get much-needed improvements done to her house and garden:

> 'When you're living on benefits, you feel like you're living on the fringes of society. But now I've got goods and services I normally couldn't have. In return I do office work for the LETS, bake cakes to order, and sell batches of vegetarian food. It makes you feel like you can actually participate.'

Her case is typical of many people living on or around the poverty line: apart from gaining access to previously unattainable goods and services, and having a chance to work, she has experienced a feeling of self-worth, and a new sense of belonging to a social network.

Changed lives

Many LETS groups contain at least one or two people who feel their lives too have been radically improved as a result of joining. Some of these have been housebound or potentially isolated. One woman living in Nottingham was suffering from ME, and used to have only one visitor a week. By joining the LETS she prompted regular visits from people coming to give help around the house, and in exchange was able to lend out items from her large record and tape library. She believed the system had changed her life.

Michael Lane, who moved to Devon 30 years ago and lives alone, was able to break through the 'incomer barrier' through joining North Devon LETS: 'We're spread across a big rural area where it's hard to get accepted unless you're a third-generation native,' he says. 'So LETS has made a community for relative newcomers such as me.'

A LETS can also be of benefit to disabled people. Ann Parnell McGarry of Brixton LETS has used the local currency to pay for a cleaner, a chiropodist, a driver, and someone to fix her computer. 'I can't imagine now how I would do without it,' she says. 'It means I can pay for all the things that social services don't provide any more.'

A system can also help people overcome a temporary crisis. When Fiona Rowson of Stroud, a single parent with a teenage son, had a knee operation and was on crutches for five months, she was able to call on fellow LETS members to help with shopping, maintaining the garden and cleaning the house. 'Having such a large network of people to draw on made a world of difference at a time when I was in great need,' she says.

In some instances LETS have come to the rescue of relationships. One couple, unemployed and with a small child, were almost at breaking point. Unable previously to afford a babysitter to help relieve the strain, through joining a LETS they were able to obtain one, an older woman living locally. She developed a good rapport with their child, enabling them to get out regularly, and their relationship soon improved. In turn they visited her, worked in her garden, and did odd jobs around her house.

For others, LETS has come at a critical moment in their emotional life. Nick Hope Wilson from the South Somerset group recalls: 'I've personally found it a lifeline. My partner left a couple of years ago, and I would have felt very isolated indeed without my work administering the LETS here.' For others again it has led to new relationships: Exeter, York and Newbury are among LETS which have brought couples together.

Yet while involvement in LETS has been a transforming experience for some, for many the benefits have been less dramatic, though nevertheless valuable. Anne Rickard, co-ordinator of Dorchester LETS, which has recruited 113 members in just over a year, sums up its value for her community:

> 'The most important factor is that it has put people in contact who wouldn't otherwise have known each other, and enabled them to help one another without having to worry about the cost. It has given them permission to ask for assistance.'

Old and new skills

LETS have helped many, particularly unemployed people, to sustain their specialist skills. Simon Lukes, co-ordinator of the 130-strong Hackney LETS, used the system to keep his hand in at plumbing. This proved crucial in his efforts to get a job. He remembers:

> 'It was my first interview for 10 years, but having kept up my skills was a tremendous confidence-booster. And because I had something else in my life with the LETS, it wasn't like there was this big abyss that I was going to fall into if I didn't get the job. But I did get it.'

But LETS have also prompted people to try out new skills, sometimes as a result of seeing an entry in the group's directory. 'You end up doing things you would never dream of doing normally,' says William Croom-Johnson, treasurer of Castle LETS in South Shropshire. As Jenny Banfield from Stroud LETS observes: 'You see people who insist they can't do anything, but then you see them change as they start trading, and often it leads to them setting up their own business.' One man from Gipping Valley LETS in Suffolk set out to sell some firewood, but found he had no takers because it was the wrong time of the year. A casual conversation during a social event revealed his love of birdwatching, and uncovered a demand for his expertise among other LETS members. Now he takes out small groups, providing them with binoculars and other equipment, and is contemplating starting his own birdwatching business.

Informal learning

Many of the larger LETS provide a wealth of learning opportunities through their members' offers of tuition in various skills or subjects. These can vary from the strictly practical to the gently philosophical, and in some places offer a programme as rich as any to be found in an adult education college.

Castle LETS, for instance, has 25 tuition listings in its directory, which include help with silk painting, public speaking, Irish history, and dog obedience training. Salisbury LETS offers 35 different educational possibilities to its 105 members, concentrating mostly on languages and the arts, and including specialisms such as Arabic, electronic music production, map reading, and Egyptian dance. Lancaster, with 238 members, has an even more dazzling array: alongside the more basic subjects such as guitar, computers and proof-reading are offers of tuition in biology, Czech, statistics, spinning, dissertation writing, ecofeminism, playing the melodeon, and motorcycle maintenance (though not Zen).

The local economy

LETS can bring many benefits to communities. They are often seen as a force for economic regeneration at local level, since they encourage people to make use of local goods and services, and both use and retain resources within the community. This is particularly true where local businesses have become involved, as they have in many systems. (See chapter 6, page 63.)

Among the 75 members of East Lothian LETS in Scotland are a picture-framing business, a removals firm, and a knitwear and jewellery shop. Jeff Terry, owner of the latter and a member of the North Berwick Trades Association, says:

> 'LETS is potentially a godsend in a place like this, where people feel if they want anything other than the basics they have to go to Edinburgh. If you know you won't have to pay the full cost of an item in cash, you're more likely to come to my shop, and I'll then take more in sterling as well as in the local currency. And as this spreads I can see huge benefits for the local cash economy too, because retailers will have more cash to spend locally.'

Trading in goods in a LETS also has the advantage of forging closer links between the producer and consumer, and enabling people to become more aware of the variety of local products available. This contrasts with the much more impersonal transactions that take place in the mainstream economy, where most products bought are from large companies based outside the local area, and shopping is a largely impersonal activity concentrating on supermarkets and superstores.

Helen Brent-Smith runs a small business in Stroud, making apple juice from local varieties. She says:

'There's much more satisfaction in selling to people you know, because they can give you feedback. People are always saying how much they miss the choice of the old varieties of apple. This way also gives them some control over what they are buying: people come back for a particular press, or say they like juice made on a particular date. It's much more satisfying for them than just going out to buy something in an anonymous place like a supermarket.'

Breaking down barriers

LETS can enhance the spirit and identity of many communities by helping to break down the barriers between existing interest groups and generations. It is an inclusive system, one that cuts across age and class barriers to embrace old and young people, the prosperous and the poor, the employed and unemployed. When it works successfully it can to some degree act as a form of extended family, encouraging people to support one another in a variety of ways.

Many LETS activities involve people working collectively, in a way that can help the community and strengthen social networks. In Manchester LETS members got together to reopen a popular Victorian Turkish baths which the council was unable to renovate. Elsewhere people have taken part in decorating gangs, run food co-operatives, helped to plant trees, run childcare parties – and of course organised a LETS trading or social event. Some of these are ambitious in scale, such as the annual six-day national LETS camps, or the 'Alter-Natives Gathering' run by members of LETS in the North of England.

Environmental benefits

A LETS can also bring environmental benefits, since its basis is sustainability. It can, for example, help to reduce pressure on the earth's finite resources. Within a LETS the sharing or loan of goods and equipment is encouraged, and the repairing and recycling of them made more affordable. People then have less need to buy costly consumer items created from scarce and non-renewable materials.

The more trading that goes on locally, involving local producers and local shops, the less need there is to bring in goods and produce from other regions or countries. Such sustainability reduces transport and fuel costs, which in turn eases the pressure on the road system. It also cuts energy costs and levels of pollution in the atmosphere, thereby contributing to the battle against global warming.

The benefits of a LETS, both tangible and intangible, are many and various. But like any scheme that involves human beings, it brings its fair share of problems. These are the subject of the next chapter.

CASE STUDY
BANBRIDGE, NORTHERN IRELAND

I t was, Margaret Glover reflects, a nightmare that turned into a happy dream. A pensioner living alone, she returned from a trip to Belfast one severely cold winter's night to find her house in Banbridge completely flooded as a result of a burst pipe. In a total panic she sought help from Mal Neumann, co-ordinator of the town's LETS:

> 'Within 20 minutes there was a team of five men at my house. The water was switched off, they took out the carpets and the bedding, they sorted out the furniture, offered me accommodation, and went on mopping everything up until four in the morning. And over the next three days they helped me sort everything out. I had no worries, they took all the stress away. It was like a miracle.'

Her story may be an extreme example of how a group of LETS members can provide an instant support network in a time of crisis. But it nevertheless sums up precisely the kind of community spirit that the system is engendering among some of the 16,000 inhabitants of this border town in the west of County Down. At the same time the group's gradual development over the last two years is just one more reflection of the desire of ordinary people in Northern Ireland to be rid of the ignorance and bigotry that has so tragically divided and damaged their country.

The 52 members of Banbridge LETS come from all backgrounds, and where religion is part of it, it is generally reckoned that they divide roughly equally between Protestant and Catholic. It undoubtedly helps the LETS cause that, despite bordering on the fervently nationalist region of South Armagh, this town standing by the banks of the Bann river is a community where people mix easily and generally live in peace – even during the marching season. Integrated schooling is available and becoming more popular – a second school is now being built. Unusually for Northern Ireland all the housing estates are genuinely mixed. For most LETS members religion is irrelevant: when the mother of one member died recently, others from different religions or none attended the service unquestioningly. 'Religion is only an excuse to start a fight,' says Kay Leckey, a painter and decorator and another LETS member. 'I don't give a damn what religion a person is. You don't even ask.' 'LETS attracts positive people, for whom those sorts of allegiances don't matter,' Mal Neumann says.

The Banbridge group also benefits from having a fair cross-section of the community as members: single parents, self-employed people, pensioners, professional couples. At one stage it included the chairman and several members of the Rotary Club: accountants, solicitors, and such like. The fact that they never traded suggested that their membership sprang more from a desire to please their chairman, who was particularly enthusiastic about the idea, than from a strong belief in the principles of the scheme. Unusually for a LETS group, although one member offers aromatherapy and massage, and two others counselling, no one is seen as 'alternative'. A large number of the offers in the directory are essentially practical: babysitting, dish washing, help with housework, grass cutting, ironing, menu planning, shopping.

Many of the transactions consist of group activities – though none are quite so unplanned as the efforts of Margaret Glover's impromptu rescue team (who were persuaded, against their wishes, to be rewarded in links, the local currency). When one woman moved to England recently, some members helped her prepare her house for sale, two drove the van all the way to Norfolk and back to keep her costs down, while others decorated her empty house and put her furniture in storage. Similarly, when the local Enterprise Centre joined and offered fax facilities, it was able to spend much of its earned links when a gang of 22 LETS members spent a day working on its gardens.

The system is a fairly relaxed and informal one, with the accounts still being handwritten from his home by Mal Neumann. 'The accounts could disappear tomorrow and the system would just carry on,' he says. 'I reckon around 80% of what people do for each other here is not recorded.' The house where he and his wife Jenny live on the edge of Banbridge tends to be the epicentre of the system, with people drifting in and out all the time. It is here that people make informal contacts that result in trading outside the directory listings: someone says they need a patio to be laid down, another person suddenly requires some wallpaper to be stripped, and arrangements are made on the spot.

For some members the social benefits are as important as any other kind. 'Mal and Jenny's door is always open, and you meet people you would never normally come into contact with,' says Ciara Clarke, a core group member. For Margaret Glover the group has evidently been a godsend:

'When I retired I became almost like a hermit, but now I've a wide circle of friends. I never feel lonely, there's always a support there. It's also broadened my thinking, it's changed my negative thoughts to positive ones. The glory of it is, you don't feel beholden, because you can reciprocate. We all have our pride and dignity, and that's very important.'

Yet like other groups, Banbridge LETS has had difficulties in spreading its message beyond the immediately enthusiastic few. 'The problem with many people is that mistrust is inbuilt,' says Ciara Clarke, who offers tuition in several languages, including Irish. 'The mindset is, What's the catch? It's so deep-rooted, there's an awfully long way to go.' People find it hard, she believes, to grasp the idea of getting something for nothing. She herself came originally from Newry, a nationalist enclave only 14 miles away, and tends to see LETS as a beacon of hope. 'It attracts more open-minded people, and that helps to bridge the gap between the two communities. That's been important for me, after my narrow upbringing. I have a dream that LETS will eventually grow big enough in Northern Ireland to make a real difference.'

For the moment, judging by what is happening elsewhere in the province, that dream looks to be a very distant one. Banbridge is one of only five LETS to have been set up in the province. In the last three years separate groups have been started in Belfast, Crumlin and Derry, while a Triangle LETS has also been established linking three towns on the northern borders of Antrim and Londonderry. But their record is a distinctly bleak one: the groups in Belfast and Derry have now ceased to exist, while the other two are only just surviving, and trading at a minimal level.

Sectarian divisions are certainly a factor in this situation, especially in Belfast, where the group finally closed down in autumn 1996 after three years' trading. 'LETS are about building and keeping trust,' says former co-ordinator Ruth Jackson, a part-time teacher. 'But suspicions go back a long, long way here – and people are right to be suspicious.' It was in order to try and break down sectarian barriers and help cross-community contacts that she and two others who initiated Belfast LETS decided to set it up on a city-wide basis, in the belief that it would be hard to find a local neighbourhood that was not predominantly either Catholic or Protestant.

Ironically, it was the 1995 ceasefire that caused the group to come under particularly intense pressure. Reporters suddenly looking for stories unconnected with the Troubles alighted on the LETS, at a time when the group was still trying to expand and develop beyond its initial 40-strong membership. Ruth Jackson remembers:

'We were naive, and not experienced enough to say we didn't want the spotlight on us at that moment. Some people said we should welcome the publicity, others felt the system wasn't sufficiently geared up to cope with all the extra interest it created. So there were divisions, and various recriminations.'

In Crumlin cross-community suspicions also played their part. A small town near Lough Neagh, often used as an overspill for Belfast, it is in an area where life is marked by a steady stream of violent incidents, aggravated more recently by a boycott of local shops. Here Jackie Forsythe, an employee of Marks & Spencer who has lived in the town for nine years, has been trying almost single-handedly to get a LETS off the ground, but has received a very muted response. She observes:

'Only seven people joined, and even those find it hard to trade with each other. People are very suspicious and insular, and also reluctant to let others do something for them. But I shall make another effort soon to get it going properly.'

In Derry, where there's generally less sectarian hostility than in Belfast, the problems in getting a LETS going were less easy to pinpoint. 'Everyone thought it was a brilliant idea, some 25 to 30 people joined, we got all the cheque books printed – but hardly anyone traded,' says former co-ordinator John Thompson. 'It didn't die a death, it just didn't have a life, and to my dying day I don't think I'll ever be sure why.'

One of the reasons for the inertia may have been to do with the way the group was set up. It was established 'from above' by a committee, which then tried to recruit members. On the face of it the group seemed to have a lot going for it: free office space in the city; a development worker with a lot of community contacts, appointed to work full time under the Action for Community Employment scheme; an official launch attended by the mayor of Derry. But the idea never properly took off, perhaps because it was never seen as a truly grass-roots organisation.

'People came to meetings, everyone was very supportive at first, we even won round the cynics who thought it was some sort of secret organisation,' John Thompson recalls. 'But then hardly any of them traded – and those that did soon became disgruntled because there were so few others doing it.' The development worker eventually left in disgust at the lack of activity, saying she didn't feel she was earning her money. After six months the system was closed down.

Various explanations for this failure have been put forward. For example, Derry has a thriving credit union, the biggest in the whole of Ireland: one possibility is that people felt membership of a community organisation with a similar self-help philosophy to that of LETS was all they needed. There again, sectarian suspicions may also have played some part in the general reluctance to trade. But in John Thompson's opinion the most likely reason is to be found in the struggle many people in the city have to scrape a living. 'You have 44% unemployment in Derry and a strong black economy,' he says. 'If people are used to having cash in hand for work they do, they're much less likely to be interested in joining a LETS.'

In contrast, one of the problems experienced in the Triangle LETS, situated over in the north-east corner of County Londonderry, seems to have had more to do with geography than history or economics. The four founding members came from four different towns – Coleraine, Castlerock, Portrush and Portstewart – and for that reason decided that one system could be set up to cover all of them. It's a decision they now believe to have been a mistake, according to one of the four, Hiller Caskey:

> 'For six months it functioned quite well. But now there's very little trading, and what there is, is very local. People are just too spread out: we now have members in Ballycastle 15 miles away, which is a problem if you don't have transport. It also destroys the point of LETS when you have to travel 20 miles or so to get a session of reflexology which you should be able to get on your doorstep.'

But the group has also encountered some resistance because of the perceived nature of its membership. The founders met at a permaculture weekend, and their initial address was the Peace Farm outside Coleraine. The farm itself joined (as did the local Quaker Meeting House), enabling members to earn local currency (the *gheegan*, the name of a local shell) by working on the farm, and spend it on items such as free-range eggs and straw. For some people, according to Hilley Casker, this gave out the wrong image:

> 'This is quite a conservative area, and people tended to see us as rather strange people who grow their own vegetables. In fact we're not strange at all, but we do all have an interest in alternative ideas. I think this has prevented us from expanding as much as we would have liked to.'

Like Jackie Forsythe in Crumlin, she looks forward to a time when interest might be revived, lessons having been learned from the initial experience. Meanwhile, in Derry and Belfast, the LETS accounts have been put into storage, in the hope that a new group will come forward to take up the challenge again. Not surprisingly, all those involved in these struggling or temporarily defunct groups are united on one point: that a LETS can really only function where there is a sizeable group of enthusiasts who have sufficient time, energy and commitment to run the system and energise the members, who can also be confident that there are others prepared to take up the baton when and if they move on.

It is a view that would apply to LETS groups everywhere, but one that seems especially pertinent to the difficult circumstances of life in Northern Ireland, where so many other obstacles face people who are trying hard to break down sectarian barriers.

THE
PROBLEMS

5

5. THE PROBLEMS

'Too many systems have been launched on a wave of enthusiasm and a few bits of paper' – a member of LETSGo

The kind of problems that arise within a LETS may be personal, economic, administrative or ideological, or a mixture of any of these. A survey of LETS groups in the UK in 1995 highlighted those experienced by the 90 groups which responded. These included:

- suspicions about the idea of LETS;
- overcoming members' fear of going into debit;
- encouraging people to trade;
- finding new members;
- fears that the trading area was too large;
- making a wider range of goods and services available.[1]

Other problems include the burn-out of core-group and founder members, the image of LETS, the question of inter-trading, and the disagreements that have arisen among LETS activists embracing different approaches.

Fears and suspicions

A significant barrier to trading is people's anxiety about dealing with strangers, whether on the phone or in person. Elizabeth Allnutt, administrator of Carlisle LETS, remembers when she started: 'When someone first rings you up and says, Will you do so and so, you think, What have I done, do I really want to do this?' Most LETS are sensitive to this concern, and some have found particular ways to alleviate it. 'We suggest people take as much care in choosing who to trade with as they do with Yellow Pages, and if possible get a personal recommendation,' says Linda Wilson, co-ordinator of Exeter LETS. 'Once people know each other there's a much greater willingness to trade.' With this in mind, Croydon LETS has recently insisted that new members attend a meeting before trading, while Brighton LETS holds a 'Joining Evening' party every two months.

With so many therapies on offer within LETS, some groups have felt it necessary to introduce safeguards within this area of trading. York LETS, which runs a self-rating star system for its directory, suggests members verify any therapist's qualifications before using their services. South-East Hampshire LETS, after holding meetings to discuss what constitutes 'a safe place' for therapists' clients, is putting together a set of Guidelines for Good Practice.

Contrary to the expectations of many outsiders or newcomers, it is very rare indeed for a system to be seriously abused by an individual. A LETS depends to a great extent on mutual trust, and examples of members being excluded for malpractice, or of going into massive debit and leaving the area, are few and far between. Much of course depends on the skills and abilities of the core group or steering committee. LETS is essentially a collective endeavour, and where too much responsibility or power is vested in one person, problems can arise.

One extreme example of this occurred in the early days of a Midlands LETS, where the self-appointed administrator was running up a large debit without the agreement of the core group. A difficult man who apparently put everyone's back up, he proved impossible to work with. Eventually an extraordinary general meeting was called in an attempt to put the group on a more collaborative footing. One of the founding members remembers the administrator's reaction to this move:

'When people tried to share out the jobs involved, he said he couldn't work with any committee, and threatened to resign. People then aired their grievances, and accused him of embezzlement. A show of hands indicated support for forming a core group – and suddenly he said he would work with it after all. However, he failed to turn up to the first meeting, at which stage it finally became clear he was trying to sabotage it. We then asked him to hand over the list of members and the accounts, but he never did. He just dropped out of the picture, and it became impossible to contact him. Perhaps we should have dug our heels in earlier, but it was very disillusioning.'

There have been a few less serious abuses. In Dorchester and other LETS members, usually self-employed, have tried to trade in sterling only. In Woodbridge in Suffolk a non-member trader tried to use the directory as a source for potential customers. Such abuses have quickly been stamped upon. In South Somerset some LETS members twice received a chain letter, inviting them to make their fortune by sending a further 20 copies to friends. 'The letter contained hidden death threats, and upset some people a lot,' says co-ordinator Nick Hope Wilson. Although the evidence suggested the letter had been sent by a LETS member misusing the directory, this was never quite proved.

Some groups have devised an arbitration or mediation process to deal with disputes. The importance of having one was underlined by an incident within Lancaster LETS, where one man was excluded by the core group for allegedly physically harassing three women. The case for exclusion was not as cut and dried as it might have been, since in each instance the woman had become emotionally involved with the man. Some LETS members, arguing that this put the incidents beyond the responsibility of the system, contested the decision. Much time and energy was expended on the appeal, which caused a good deal of bad feeling in and around the town. 'It was very hairy and could have destroyed the system, it brought out a lot of conflict,' says co-ordinator Sue Cowgill. 'But we felt that if we ignored that kind of thing, we'd be colluding.'

The conflict prompted Lancaster LETS to reassess and overhaul its complaints procedure, and to establish a mediation group as the first point of reference for members with complaints. Several groups have now introduced such a mechanism as a safeguard. In the rare cases where mediation has been necessary, it has generally been used to try to settle a disagreement about the quality of work done in a transaction.

In theory, responsibility for all aspects of a LETS transaction rests with the two parties concerned, and most groups have a clause in their members' agreement which makes it clear that the quality of work done or goods exchanged is no concern of the administration. But in practice the demarcation line can become blurred. In South Powys there was a dispute over the sale of a car within the system, though the case was complicated by the fact that no formal complaint was made for several months, by which time the alleged villain was no longer a member. There was disagreement in the group as to whether the administration should become involved. 'If you get done by a builder, you don't go to the Bank of England,' was the argument of one member. But John Rogers, who did eventually mediate, believes it was the right thing to do. 'It was about keeping relations good,' he recalls. 'We didn't want people thinking LETS means you get ripped off. It's important that these problems are known about, that people don't just sit on them.'

Going into debit

One of the most widespread problems, which seems to affect a great many people when they first join a LETS, is the worry about being 'in debt'. It takes a while for existing members to convince newcomers that the system will actually benefit if they go into debit early on, because by doing so they are stimulating trade. Many people don't find it easy to grasp the principle that the 'debt' is to the community rather than to an individual. Even when they understand that no interest will be incurred, they are often still reluctant to take that first step. 'This worry about going into debit is the biggest barrier of all to successful trading,' says Linda Wilson, co-ordinator of Exeter LETS. 'New members often just sit by the phone and wait for it to ring.'

Encouraging trade

Another obstacle is people's conviction, either before or after joining a group, that they do not have anything to offer. This invariably turns out to be untrue, since there are certain basic jobs – house sitting, dog walking, providing car lifts – which almost anyone can manage. Pressed by a LETS co-ordinator to compile a list of their skills, many people discover to their surprise that they have half a dozen services or goods that they can offer to others.

Trading levels vary enormously between groups, but in a good many just a minority are active – the all-too-common situation of 20% of the people doing 80% of the work is frequently mentioned. A survey of six LETS in Cornwall revealed active trading to vary from 17% to 70% of the membership.[2] Yet maintaining a decent level of trading is crucial to the success of a group.

This can be significantly affected by people's motives for joining. Those who do so for practical or economic reasons, perhaps with an eye to getting their bedroom redecorated or their bicycle mended without delay, will quite likely start trading immediately. Those who sign up because they like the principle of LETS may prove more reluctant, as has happened in Carlisle. As Elizabeth Allnutt admits:

'None of us really trades enough. People don't actually need the system, they just think, "What a good idea, let's join," rather than make a point of seeing what's on offer. The only person who trades properly is a woman whose husband is on sick pay, who uses it to supplement her income. The rest of us think it's a jolly good idea, but it's a philosophical rather than a practical conviction.'

Some groups have created special incentives to help people trade. Richmond and District LETS in North Yorkshire, for instance, offers a reward to the biggest spender in each quarterly period, while Falmouth LETS runs regular trading competitions.

Keeping and finding members

Many groups find it difficult to retain members in areas where the population is particularly mobile, and where the sense of community is consequently weakest. Earl's Court in West London is a classic example of this problem. An area with a constantly shifting multi-ethnic population, its inhabitants include itinerant backpackers, and many refugees newly arrived in the UK. A LETS was started in 1994, but by spring 1997 it still had only some 25 members.

Niki Kortvelyessy, its co-ordinator, says:

'It's always spluttered, and I've had to relaunch it every now and then. There really isn't a community here, and we don't have the resources or even the ideas for building one. There are a lot of small needs, but these are generally dealt with by the local community centre.'

She admits that very little trading is going on at present:

'That's partly to do with size, but also the narrow range of trading possibilities. Everyone seems to want computer classes, and there's none of the therapies and suchlike that you get in most LETS.'

At the most recent relaunch meeting, a couple of Asian members of the community centre described LETS as 'a great con', while a group of Bosnian refugees, some of them highly qualified, were extremely keen on the idea. Niki Kortvelyessy recalls:

'They could see the point of it ideologically. The LETS principle was familiar to them, it reminded them of a similar system operating in their own country. However, although they were initially very enthusiastic and joined, they've hardly traded at all.'

Local or beyond?

One problem for many groups is to decide on the geographical boundaries of their operation. This is a particularly thorny issue in rural areas. Typically a group may be set up in a cluster of villages or in a town, and after a while begin to attract members from further afield. Then comes a moment when a decision has to be made whether or not to set up new groups in these other places. Clearly much depends on whether distance is proving a barrier to people trading, and the level of enthusiasm for LETS in these 'new' areas.

Penzance LETS in Cornwall is one that is currently facing this dilemma. Its operation takes in towns such as St Ives, Hayle and St Just, none of them more than 10 miles away. Co-ordinator Mary MacArthur says:

'It's a development we'd like to see happen. Our group is still growing, so we're hoping that people will start up a LETS in those towns, even if we still do the accounting centrally. We plan to hold an information evening in each place, and play the LETS game to stimulate additional interest.'

But the problem is not confined to rural areas, though in large towns and cities the dilemma is of a different order. In London attempts have been made to group LETS on a regional basis, for instance in North London. But these have not proved wholly successful, since many members seem to prefer to limit their trading to their own area rather than go even a few miles in such a densely populated place. As one sceptic put it: 'If I live in Islington, I don't want to go all the way to Barnet to have my hair cut.'

The core group burn-out

Some groups run into more subtle difficulties after a few years. The initial obstacles have been overcome, the membership is well established, the system is ticking over smoothly, but the pioneering spirit has evaporated. The group seems in need of new blood, of fresh ideas. This is what has happened within

Salisbury LETS, according to co-ordinator Mandy Goddard:

> 'While experience and efficiency have increased, I for one feel this is no longer enough. The vital ingredient of enthusiasm is slowly ebbing away from all of us. At our monthly meeting you find four or five people desperately trying to drum up the enthusiasm to get through the evening's business without glancing at their watches every five minutes. It's a familiar tale: the same few people do most of the work most of the time, and they carry on because nobody else volunteers to take over. People get burned out, and sometimes just grind to a halt.'

The image of LETS

Problems can also be caused by people's varying perceptions of a LETS and what it can offer them. Many directories, especially those in small towns and rural areas, are awash with alternative therapies, conjuring up a vision of the entire membership devoting all their waking hours to massaging and counselling each other. Groups are often seen simply as part of the alternative culture, and therefore somehow not respectable. As one member of Carlisle LETS observes: 'My husband thinks I shouldn't be playing around with something like this, that I'm simply a sub-hippie.' People's needs depend of course on their personal circumstances and income level. One member of South Somerset LETS complained that 'the essentials of life as needed by the unemployed are not available', and that the group was 'just a cosy club trading in trivia'.

People's initial perceptions often depend on the kind of language used to advertise or promote a group. Much of the early publicity was put out by people with a special interest in the theory of money, interest and local currencies, who were unable to avoid using jargon. Classic examples of this were uncovered by researchers in the initial literature put out by LETS advocates targeting estates in Manchester and Glasgow. The researchers observed:

> 'Such language was especially alienating in the areas we visited. The idea that "money is just information" is highly abstract. The further idea that since information is free, so is money, simply does not speak to inner-city

residents who have been struggling to make ends meet all their lives. They do not have the time – or the money – to play with such philosophical arguments.'[3]

Inter-trading

Opinion is divided on the desirability of inter-trading. Some people believe that the beauty of a LETS system is its very localness, the fact that it is rooted in a particular community, and that inter-trading inevitably lessens its value. Others feel that if LETS is to develop as an alternative economy alongside the mainstream one, then inter-trading is essential.

Many see inter-trading as an obvious way of providing access to a wider range of goods and services. In Suffolk such a view has led to the adoption of a county-wide LETS (see page 93). York LETS, with over 200 members, recently decided to inter-trade with Ryedale LETS, with only 40 members, so that they could get access to goods and services of a slightly more rural nature – for instance, a tractor trailer or a holiday home on the Moors. But others feel that such benefits are outweighed by the potential administrative complications, or the danger of local transactions suffering as a result of these wider opportunities.

Nic Evans, of Totnes LETS, believes such obstacles can be overcome:

'Inter-LETS trading is not meant to supplant local trading. More likely it would supplement a larger volume of local trade. Yes, a LETS is delightfully local and community based – but LETS don't advocate the isolation of communities, nor suggest that a community can be totally self-sufficient. There is an atmosphere of co-operation between LETS: so why not trade?'[4]

One of the more problematic area of LETS activity is the involvement of businesses, which is dealt with separately in the next chapter.

CASE STUDY
GLASGOW, SCOTLAND

The first business on the agenda was the forthcoming *ceilidh* in the local Baptist church hall. The discussion was lively. How much should people have to pay to enter? What mixture of groats and sterling should they be charged? Should unemployed members be allowed a discount, or should everyone in the group be treated equally?

These and other crucial details having been hammered out, the meeting of the West Glasgow LETS steering group – designer Mo Macleod, environmental worker Ron Senior and business consultant Patrick Boase – moved on to other matters. They discussed the content of their next newsletter, looked at some of the problems involved in the running of the new wholefood bulk-buying scheme, and decided that the largish debt incurred by one member who had just moved away didn't actually create a problem for the system.

It was a typical run-of-the-mill get-together of the steering group, held on this occasion in the sitting room of Patrick Boase's elegant Victorian house in Partick. Yet the detailed nuts-and-bolts work done at this kind of session is clearly crucial to the successful running of one of the most active LETS groups in Scotland.

Set up in 1993, West Glasgow LETS covers the Partick, Dowanhill, Hyndland and Broomhill areas of the city, and has 60 members. One of them is Fred Greer, a single mother living on income support. She's used the system for babysitting, lifts, haircutting, bike maintenance and legal advice. 'I joined LETS mainly for financial reasons, and it's been pretty useful for me, it's made my life easier,' she says. Nevertheless there are some problems:

> 'It's actually a very middle-class group: the directory has lots of word-processing on offer, but not much plumbing. And it's not that well known except among trendy lefties in the area: I hardly ever get phoned by anyone that doesn't already know me. There are a few working-class people, but they're not very typical, they've usually been to university.'

West Glasgow is one of six LETS groups to have been established in the city. Four of the others are based in Kelvingrove, Southside, Townhead and Drumchapel, while a fifth, Quines LETS, covers the whole of Glasgow. The challenges and problems are different for each, depending to a large extent on the nature of the area, the kind of lives people lead and, perhaps most critically of all, the level of commitment and enthusiasm of those who administer the group.

Quines LETS is something of a special case, since it allows only women to join ('quine' means woman in Scots). Sitting in the recently opened Insomnia Gallery in West Glasgow, the city's first 24-hour café, co-ordinator Jude Stewart underlines the group's philosophy:

> 'It's not a group against men, it's one that's for women. We set it up because some women were not very keen to have a strange man come in to the house. We also wanted to encourage women to learn things like plumbing and other skills usually monopolised by men.'

The group got off the ground in 1994, and has around 30 members. Although a series of planned workshops on plumbing and other traditionally male jobs never actually took place, it seems to have been moderately successful in other ways. It has attracted a cross-section of women who have traded with each other from different parts of the city, and has resulted in several permanent friendships. Recently there were rumours that it had closed down. In reality it had been treading water as a result of an administrative crisis. 'We had a core group of six women, but all of us got ill, life took over, and our administration died a death,' Jude Stewart says. 'Now it needs a new life, and we're hoping it will rise again.'

Kelvingrove LETS, based in the area of Glasgow University, has also lost some of its founder members. It has nevertheless managed to maintain a steady flow of trading since it was founded, and now has close on 100 members. Charles Kennedy, one of the original group, says:

> 'I don't know who most of them are any more. Many of those who were in at the start, some of them environmental or permaculture people, joined for ideological reasons, and have rather faded away now. It's also a very mobile population, people move around a lot even within the same area. But the group still manages to regenerate itself and grow. Two-thirds of the members have traded in the last year, even though a quarter are new to the group.'

While West Glasgow and Kelvingrove LETS are apparently thriving, the LETS on the Drumchapel Estate on the outskirts of Glasgow has had a much more chequered history. Built in the 1950s, the estate houses 12,000 people, and has had immense problems with drug dealing, alcohol dependency, and poor health and diet. In the past it has been the target for many community initiatives set up by outside agencies, and with a credit union, a food co-op and a health project already in place, would seem to be the kind of place that would give a warm welcome to a LETS.

But the group, formally launched in 1994, has never really got going. The handful of local people who started it up were also heavily involved in other projects, and found they had insufficient time to do the crucial development work on the system. They recruited only 15 members, and little trading took place. One barrier to recruitment may have been the fact that the LETS was begun by activists in two men's groups on the estate, and until recently the membership was wholly male. Another factor was the concern over the legal position with benefits, and a good deal of the first year was spent getting legal advice on this question.

Charles Kennedy, who visited the estate to talk about his experience of LETS, believes this approach was wrong:

> 'They wasted two years in committee-type discussions. I said to them, Just do it. But they kept thinking you needed a lot of money and plenty of computers. I tried to point out that they didn't, and that anyway they had more access to computers than we did.'

Patrick Boase makes a similar point. 'They threw a spanner in the works because they made it sound much more complicated than it was.'

The development of Drumchapel LETS was not helped when two key members who were unemployed suddenly got jobs, and were unable to give the administrative work the attention it needed. Security was also a potential issue when it came to getting a system started, since anyone visiting a house on the estate has to seek police authorisation. Since LETS trading is done by appointment between individuals this was not necessarily seen as a problem, but the LETS core group nevertheless decided to issue people with identity cards as proof of membership.

Despite these difficulties, it does seem that Drumchapel LETS might be revived. It was relaunched in late 1996 with a new committee, and a new membership list which now includes women. There are also hopes that a development worker can be funded. 'It's important to have someone who can devote all their time to running and developing the system,' says co-ordinator Mary Malcolmson. 'If we can get that I think it will take off.'

Since LETS first got going in Scotland some 50 groups have been established, of which around 35 were reckoned to be still in existence by spring 1997. There are several reasons why groups have failed, but there seems to be a consensus that a minimum of around 30 members is needed for trading to be viable. Success also seems to depend on having a varied membership. One suburban LETS started by a group of young mothers built up a good network among themselves, but lacked a sufficient range of skills to provide a broad enough base for trading, and eventually closed down.

The basic need to share the load of running a group is underlined by the experience of Flora Selwyn, co-ordinator of the St Andrews LETS in Fife, which has 32 paid-up members. She appears to have taken the lion's share of responsibility for keeping the group going:

> 'It definitely needs more than one or even two committed people to run a LETS. Recently I have been in a mood to quit. Two years of not very obvious progress seems a long time. It might of course be all my fault, but I had hoped someone would oust me and get on with it.'

Recent discussions about amalgamating with two other small neighbouring groups, in Cupar (23 members) and East Neuk (18 members), seemed to offer real hope of progress.

> 'But then the enthusiastic member who volunteered to design the new directory incorporating all three groups vanished without trace, so our optimism was a trifle misplaced.'

The St Andrews LETS is one of the smallest in Scotland; the largest is in Stirling, with 120 members. With a proper administrative office, Stirling LETS has been able to organise and stage national events, including a conference entitled 'Could a Local Currency Revive Your Community?' aimed at people in community organisations and local authorities. The amount of contact LETS groups have had with their local councils has varied greatly. By no means all of the groups want their help. Jayne Taylor of Kelvingrove LETS, which has had money from Strathclyde Regional Council to finance the printing of their leaflets, says: 'A LETS group shouldn't need that kind of support, because if you get it, there's a danger you end up being beholden to them.'

Many groups have found that local businesses are reluctant to join because they see no obvious benefit in doing so. East Lothian LETS, now in its third year, has had some success in overcoming their resistance. Among its 75 members are a picture-framing business and a removals firm, both in Dunbar, and Antiok, a knitwear and jewellery shop in North Berwick. Between them they allow LETS members to pay 20 to 30% of the price of their goods and services in ellets, the local currency.

Jeff Terry, the owner of Antiok and a member of North Berwick's Trades Association, believes LETS makes obvious sense for local businesses:

'LETS is potentially a godsend in a place like this, where people feel if they want anything other than the basics they have to get in the car and go to Edinburgh. If you know you won't have to pay the full cost of an item in cash, you're more likely to come to my shop, and I'll then take more in cash as well as ellets. I'll then use the ellets to pay staff who are LETS members, or pay local suppliers. As this spreads I can see huge benefits for the local cash economy too, because retailers will have more cash to spend locally.'

While the size of a group is an important factor, so too are geography and distance. Most people prefer to trade reasonably locally, but some positively welcome the chance to go further afield. This is certainly the case in East Lothian LETS, which covers an area of nearly 300 square miles, embracing a number of small towns but also a large rural hinterland. 'We haven't wanted to split into smaller units, as people enjoy having a wider area to trade in,' says co-ordinator Sheena Anthony. 'They've also made friends outside their local area that they would otherwise not have made.' In order to ensure that people keep in touch, the group publishes a monthly newsletter with details of new members.

A few groups in Scotland are necessarily self-contained because of geographical barriers; examples are those that have been operating on the island of Arran in the west, and the Shetland Islands in the far north. In both cases half the population consists of newcomers, who have generally been the ones to get involved. On Arran the LETS has grown to 57 members in two years. 'Some local folk are involved, but it mainly appeals to people who see trading as a lifestyle or philosophical statement, and who may not be so concerned about the benefits it can bring,' says co-ordinator Richard Lane.

On Shetland there is also considerable caution. In three-and-a-half years 50 people have joined, but trading, which is in terns ('One good tern ... '), is slow. 'I think the further north you go, the more cautious people are about LETS,' says co-ordinator Peter Bevington. He compares the response on Shetland since he arrived three years ago with the flood of enthusiasm and excitement LETS generated in Australia when he was there:

> 'A lot of people here are waiting on the sidelines: they're interested and supportive, but they won't join in, they want to see it working first. Some of them haven't quite grasped what it's about. It's Catch 22, and we're having to learn a lot of patience. But it feels positive, the core is growing, and that gives me confidence.'

A crucial role in the development of LETS around the country has been played by the national body LetsLink Scotland, modelled on LetsLink UK. It provides information and advice through a system of regional co-ordinators, runs conferences, sells publications and raises money. It does not promote any particular LETS model, but exists to encourage diversity and experimentation. A particular emphasis is put on the need for groups which join to retain their autonomy.

Lesley Rowan, until recently its administrator, says:

> 'We've been going for three years and have barely scratched the surface. But the quality and diversity of the people who have become involved has been impressive.'

An application for charitable status was recently rejected by the Inland Revenue (there is no Charity Commission in Scotland), on the grounds that helping disadvantaged communities was not a charitable purpose. Now an application is being made for lottery funding for one year, so that regional co-ordinators can be trained, and be paid to help local groups. Patrick Boase, the new Co-ordinator of LetsLink Scotland, says:

> 'There's been a lot of waste in the past, with groups failing and shutting up shop. If assistance could be available it would make a great difference. There's enough people around now who know how to do it. With this

kind of community development I think you either need existing networks, or people who are skilled at creating them.'

The third national LETS conference was held on the island of Arran in autumn 1996. Attended by over a hundred LETS activists, it apparently proved a source of inspiration to many, enabling people to share experiences and ideas from different areas of the country. Workshops such as that entitled 'Thirty Members – Now What?' provided a range of practical ideas on how to run a successful LETS. There was also a lively discussion on the planned Free University for Scotland, a utopian idea which has recently provoked much debate, and which seemed to link in with several LETS ideas about flexible learning, peripatetic teachers, and skills exchange.

Perhaps the most ambitious plan yet, in a country with a relatively small population dispersed over a large area, is the proposed nationwide LETS, based on Michael Linton's MultiLETS idea. This is to be known as ScotLETS, and its unit of currency would be the scotia. 'Its potential is great,' says Mark Ruskell, LETS regional contact for Lothian and the Borders. 'It would enable people to make use of services such as holiday accommodation, or to get hold of genuine local goods, such as Fair Isle sweaters, without having to use sterling.'

GETTING
THE
BUSINESS

6

6. GETTING THE BUSINESS

'Eyes light up in the business world when they hear about the
WIR idea' – David Williams, West London Interest Free Trading

The question of the involvement of businesses in LETS is a complex one, and the subject of a great deal of discussion in the LETS world. Those groups that have attempted to bring businesses into their systems have found it a hard nut to crack.

Some people believe that persuading businesses to join is essential if the aim is to develop and expand, and so offer people a wider range of goods and services than they can get from individual members. They point to schemes in other countries which do so and enable cars, houses and mortgages to be available on a system. Others have no particular desire for business involvement in what they see as primarily a social network. Some have found from experience that the difficulties involved in getting businesses to participate are not worth the trouble taken. Meanwhile, businesses themselves are often uncertain or sceptical about the value of belonging to a LETS, and several have withdrawn after sampling the system.

The vast majority that have already joined a LETS are small businesses or sole traders. Most are self-employed people, often working from home. Many building-based businesses that have joined are seen as 'green' or 'alternative'. Several wholefood cafés or shops have signed up – for example in Bradford, Chagford on Dartmoor, Hackney, Kingston and Stroud; fair trading shops in Bristol and Bradford-on-Avon belong to local groups; a New Age bookshop has joined the LETS in Exeter; a woodland coppicing company the one in Calderdale. But in certain places more conventional businesses – accountants, solicitors, pubs and hotels – have also become involved.

In theory a LETS can offer a business a range of benefits. These include:

- free and instant credit, reducing the amount they need to borrow for those starting up a business;
- a price advantage over competitors, which can help to expand the number of customers or clients, and increase income;
- free publicity through the LETS directory and newsletters;
- an opportunity to try out new products or services without spending

national currency;

- an increase in the amount of national currency it has available, since basic goods or services can be paid for in the local currency;
- the possibility of accepting payment in a mixture of local and national currency, to cover expenditure on overheads;
- a chance to enhance its reputation in the community by supporting a system that keeps economic activity local.

However, persuading businesses to join a LETS can be very difficult, and some groups have given up on the idea. A typical experience is that of Dorchester LETS, which was set up in late 1994, has around 90 members, and trades in marts. In its early days it printed a special leaflet for potential business members, outlining the benefits to be gained, the arrangements for paying partly in sterling and partly in marts, and the position on tax and VAT. However, only a handful actually joined: of these one has since withdrawn, and another, a local pub, is only offering food on a 10% LETS basis, an offer that few LETS members have taken up.

Anne Rickard, Dorchester's co-ordinator, recalls some of the obstacles:

'Originally we had all sorts of hopes, but they've not really worked out. It's no good if a business is half-hearted about the idea, they have to be really committed. A lot of them think a LETS is a good idea in principle, but are not sure how it's going to work out in practice – for example how they're going to spend their local currency. There was also the question of reliability: businesses need to get what they want when they want it, and that's not always possible when they trade with individual LETS members.'

This problem of being able to spend local currency is a key one. There are many examples of businesses losing their initial enthusiasm or dropping out of a system for this reason. Liz Shephard of LetsLink UK highlights one part of the problem:

'We've always been in favour of businesses joining a LETS, because ultimately it's about economic development. But you have to be careful in the early stages, since it's often green businesses, which tend to be struggling, that are the ones to get on board first. But if the LETS group is not sufficiently large, they can amass large amounts of credit, and not have the corresponding purchasing power.'

The group that appears to have been the most successful on this front is Manchester LETS, which has run conferences specifically to sell the idea to businesses. The system currently has 65 small businesses on its books. Most are sole traders, but the list also includes a grocery/food co-operative, a cycle shop, an Internet café, two businesses involved in recycling, an accountant, a solicitor, a vegetarian café, a taxi firm, a garden centre, and an architectural practice. At one stage a separate LETS was launched based on a black business network in Moss Side, with the aim of encouraging black enterprise. Despite a lot of enthusiasm, this never really got going, and when the network folded the LETS did also – although some of the businesses then joined Manchester LETS.

Businesses obviously need to be convinced that joining will be of benefit to them, but they can easily be put off if the whole idea seems too complicated. Some LETS activists believe they need training before joining a LETS. One of these is Les Moore of the LETSGo organisation who, armed with a small grant from the City Challenge budget, is hoping to set up a LETS specifically for small businesses in Dalston, North London. While he has had expressions of interest from 20 in the area – including a solicitor, a training provider, a driving school, a vegetarian café, and an Internet supplier – they have yet to sign up formally to the scheme:

> 'You find business advisers are very keen and supportive, but businesses one-to-one are a bit cooler. There's a danger that they see the effort they need to put in as being out of all proportion to the benefits they will gain. Their attention span is only so long, and if it gets too complicated for them, they turn off. Ideally what you need is to be able to spend four or five hours with them, and explain the idea very carefully.'

A more complex and ambitious scheme has just been launched in West London by David Williams, who now works as an independent LETS consultant after a stint as LETS development officer for the London Borough of Hounslow. (See case study, page 29.) West London Interest-Free Trading (WestLIFT), aimed at businesses in Ealing, Hillingdon and Hounslow, is being funded for three years by the European Government Office for London, to the tune of £100,000 annually.

The scheme is modelled on a celebrated organisation which has been operating in Switzerland since 1934. WIR – Wirtschaftsring (Economic

Circle) – is an independent currency system for small and medium-sized businesses which now has some 80,000 account-holders, and is bringing in new members at the rate of 100 a month. It is a non-profit-making co-operative owned by its members, with a massive directory of services, and a substantial guide listing hotels and restaurants all over the country that take part-payment in WIR currency. The sheer size of the operation is breathtaking: a recent directory listed 1,853 architects, 167 lawyers, 16 undertakers and a circus.

The targets for WestLIFT are rather more modest: David Williams hopes that 250 businesses will sign up in the first year, and 500 in the second. The scheme will allow members to decide for themselves what proportion of WestLIFT currency they are prepared to accept for particular goods or services, taking into account high and low trading periods. It will also enable existing members to act as guarantors for new businesses that are too young to get a satisfactory credit reference from the bank.

David Williams believes that members offering skilled, professional services could particularly benefit. He suggests:

> 'They can charge everyone the same rate, but agree to accept different methods of payment from a variety of clients, depending on the demand. For instance, a graphic artist who regularly gets two full days' work per week may be very willing to offer one full day on WestLIFT currency, or accept 30% in the currency if this was leading to a greater volume of work and an increase in cash income.'

He points out that WestLIFT is not aiming to become a substitute for cash, but could provide a way for businesses to maximise their trading.

Businesses as well as individuals are often wary of joining a LETS because of uncertainties about the tax and trading implications. The next chapter examines these, as well as the crucial issue of benefits.

CASE STUDY
SOUTH POWYS, WALES

Few communities can boast such a high proportion of LETS members as the hamlet of Tretower in Wales. Tucked into a stunningly beautiful valley near the Black Mountains in the Brecon Beacons, it has a population of just 50 people, of whom six are members of South Powys LETS.

One of these is Tony Care, who has been in the system since it started four years ago. Severely physically disabled by an accident, he uses a crutch to get around, and so has to rely on others for heavy physical work such as painting windows, building a pond or spreading compost in the ample garden at the side of his house. 'Living on a low income, I couldn't normally afford to employ someone to do that kind of work,' he says, as he sits talking in his cheerfully cluttered stone-floor kitchen. 'With LETS I can, so it makes me feel quite wealthy.'

From the 300 year-old converted dairy he shares with Odile Troffigue and their 15 year-old daughter, he is able to offer a range of useful goods and services to earn enough beacons (the South Powys currency) to pay for this physical work to be done by other LETS members. He grinds flour for home baking, sharpens many varieties of gardening tools, and hires out unusual items such as a compost shredder, a juice extractor, and a large marquee. Meanwhile his partner, who comes from Brittany and is also a LETS member, offers French lessons and translating work.

Tony Care agrees that he and other LETS folk who live nearby – his mother is next door, three others are just across the road – would probably help each other out in such ways even if the system didn't exist. 'But when it's formalised like this you find out all sorts of things that people can do, and it gives you a chance to flaunt your own skills,' he observes.

There's certainly a varied range of skills listed in the South Powys directory. Alongside the usual kind of goods and services offered and required by most LETS groups are several tending towards the exotic: Moroccan vegetarian meals, body-mind centering, junk percussion workshops, dog jackets made to order, horse minding, advice on cycling posture, and Sanskrit for beginners. Little of this, it would appear, is of interest to the families who have been here for generations, as opposed to incomers such as Tony Care who has lived in the area for 25 years:

> 'Most LETS members, whether they're Welsh or English, have moved in
> from elsewhere. None of the local people have joined. Most of them are

farmers, or come from farming families. But then they've always run a kind of neighbourhood exchange, so they probably see less reason to join a LETS.'

A long, narrow county stretching from north to south through the middle of Wales, Powys contains breathtaking landscape, and is still relatively unspoilt. Some LETS members have been helping to keep it that way. In Painscastle, where one woman planned to resurrect a derelict barn, she was able to afford to employ a professional to build a traditional retaining wall, because half of his £1,000 fee could be paid in beacons. The craftsman also spent a day training other LETS members in the skill. 'It's wonderful that LETS can be used to keep the landscape right,' says Eluned Hurn, a South Powys founder member. 'So many people come here and make it look like Bexhill.'

Powys has five LETS groups, based in Aberystwyth, Presteigne, Llanidloes, Mid Powys and South Powys. John Rogers, a teacher and trainer, co-ordinates the latter group from the front room of his house in Bronllys, which doubles as a LETS office. He admits that it is not easy to persuade people to join: 'It's a very conservative area, and attitudes change very slowly. People still have a lingering suspicion of LETS, that somehow it's illegal, or part of the black economy. So the majority of our members are incomers – though some of them have actually been here many years.'

The nature of the group's membership has proved a problem in its attempts to get financial help. When it applied in 1995 for European money to help promote the system, a report commissioned by the potential funding organisation concluded that the LETS was mainly for the benefit of English incomers, and was one that made little real impact on the indigenous population. This decision upset John Rogers: 'I was really incensed, because they'd totally missed the point. The money would have helped us to work with the local authority and make more people aware of the system. As it is, we've got nowhere with the council.'

There has been one small but possibly significant recognition of the value of the system by the local authority. The group has had its first referral from social services, of a self-employed scrap dealer and haulage contractor. This man had got by for many years on a low income, but suddenly found himself in financial difficulties. 'Social services thought we might be able to help him,' John Rogers says. 'When he came to us he was in despair. He was beginning to think the conventional system was there to wipe him out.'

Meanwhile the group has started to work with local welfare organisations such as the Brecon Unemployed Self-Help Association and People in Partnership, an advocacy organisation for people in hospital. Membership has also extended to the local branch of Tools for Self-Reliance, the Arts Alive community arts group, and the telecottage in the high school in Crickhowell.

One novel element of trading in South Powys is the group's community development account, which awards grants in beacons to people who are organising an event, project or course which uses the goods and services of its members within the region. John Rogers explains:

> 'We decided we were being too cautious about the system's own account being in debt. If LETS is to be truly radical, we need to work on the basis of "Whatever needs doing, let's get it done". So, for example, we've spent hundreds of beacons on a major professional revamp of our directory. Previously we would have seen that as something we could not afford. Of course we're very aware of the danger of creating inflation, but we're just going to see how it works out.'

The scheme was started in 1996, and three grants have so far been awarded. One grateful recipient has been Caroline Mackenzie, a woodcut artist who for the last four years has organised a May Day Festival in the forest near Llaneglwys. 'These events take a lot of time to set up, and I was doing it on my own for nothing,' she says. In 1996, armed with a grant of 100 beacons, she was able to use the currency to hire a marquee for the first time, to get various forms of help from other LETS members, and to reimburse herself for the time spent organising the festival.

The South Powys group operates within a radius of some 35 miles, extending from Rhayader to Abergavenny. Like other groups where members are widely scattered, it is looking at ways of improving trading within as well as between the different communities. To this end it has begun to appoint local co-ordinators to organise local events and seek out new members. Individuals have already taken on this role in Brecon, Hay-on-Wye, Crickhowell and Abergavenny. 'We need to encourage the core to get stronger in each locality,' John Rogers argues. 'Eventually we would hope to have half a dozen mini-LETS, though the accounting would still be done centrally.'

While trading is relatively brisk in South Powys despite the geographical barriers, it appears to be less buoyant among the 100 or so members of the Vale of Clwyd LETS in North Wales. Part of the problem here seems to be the tendency of many members to join in a rush of enthusiasm, and then find in practice that they have little time to trade. This in turn causes frustration among other members, who discover that 'offers' listed in the directory turn out to be no longer valid. One new member recently made 10 contacts before being able to find what he was looking for.

Trading is also in the doldrums within the LETS group in Haverfordwest, Pembrokeshire, one of the first to be set up in Wales in 1993 (the first was in neighbouring Narberth). 'We have a few stalwarts, but little trading goes on at present,' admits Frank Hippman, a committee member. This seems a far cry from the group's optimistic beginnings in 1993.

At the time Harry Wears, one of the moving spirits in a founding group of a couple of dozen enthusiasts, had somewhat grand plans to recruit as many as 2,000 members. For a while the group grew quite rapidly, and encompassed all social classes. It also included a significant number of unemployed people – at one stage they comprised as much as 70% of the membership. One of the aims was to bring in businesses, especially those just starting up, or any that were thinking of laying people off. One of the more ambitious plans was to refurbish a disused local school and reopen it as a day nursery, using the project as a training ground for unemployed people wanting to get into the building construction business. The scheme would enable them to work without risk of losing any benefit, and simultaneously gain some useful qualifications.

A few businesses did sign up to the scheme, including a pub and the local branch of the Co-op. The latter started trading by buying items to give as prizes for the school competitions they were promoting, and offering services to the group's administration. A music venue in Narberth joined up, enabling LETS members to pay for tickets partly in sterling and partly in LETS. But most of the plans never quite came to fruition. The owners of the local school decided to put the property on the open market. The pub dropped out of the system. Even the Co-op, after its initial enthusiasm, withdrew: 'It was a decision by someone in the higher echelons of the organisation,' Frank Hippman explains. 'They decided that if the Haverfordwest Co-op joined a LETS, then all their other branches would have to do so too.'

Trading has also temporarily ground to a halt in Swansea, where a LETS group, consisting principally of employed middle-class people living or working in the city, was established in 1995, eventually recruiting 60 members. While the standstill has come about partly because key people have moved away, it has also been caused by changes in funding arrangements affecting the local community development agency. However, according to former co-ordinator Susan Stockwell, a rebirth is on the cards: 'We hope soon to rise phoenix-like from the ashes, but now it will be more down to the membership to do what people want.' Meanwhile there are moves to set up a group on the city's Townhill Estate, which is notorious for car theft and lack of policing, and where it is thought a LETS could have a role.

The Welsh language appears not to have been a significant issue in the operation of LETS groups around Wales, even in a Welsh-speaking area such as the Vale of Clwyd. Helen Melvin, an English incomer from Cumbria, says there are only a handful of Welsh-speaking members, and virtually no demand for bilingual printed material – although they do trade in *ddraigs* (dragons). Ironically, the group will soon be producing leaflets and newsletters in Welsh as well as in English if it succeeds in its application for £2,000 of European money via Denbighshire council, which insists on such a commitment as a condition of giving the money.

Involving councils in LETS was one of the many aims of the first Wales and the Marches regional conference, held in Talgarth in June 1995, and attended by several council representatives as well as members from 25 LETS groups from Wales, and the border counties such as Shropshire and Herefordshire. The occasion also marked the first serious discussion about the possibility of co-ordinating the work of groups nationwide. Among the ideas floated were the creation of a Welsh directory, a LetsLink for the whole principality based on the UK LetsLink model, an all-Wales trade fair, and an all-Wales LETS for inter-trading.

However, although three committees were established to take forward these and other ideas, very little has been put into practice since. Plans such as those for a Welsh LetsLink, for example, have been stillborn because of a lack of funding, leaving groups to continue to rely on informal contacts across the far-flung regions of the principality.

LEGAL MATTERS

7. LEGAL MATTERS

'We want tax paid in sterling: the chancellor will not appreciate having his lawn mowed' – Inland Revenue spokeswoman

The question of the exact relationship between LETS and the tax and welfare systems is crucial to its growth and development. Already it is having an impact on systems around the UK. Many people are understandably extremely wary of joining a LETS because of a belief that their earnings or benefits may be adversely affected. Yet experience so far suggests that the fear of earnings or benefits loss is far greater than any actual loss.

The benefits question

Much of the uncertainty over benefits stems from the failure of the UK government to issue clear, comprehensive and consistent guidelines on the effect of LETS incomes on benefit levels. There seems in recent times to have been little awareness of LETS on the part of the Department of Social Security (DSS), which in general assumes an attitude of 'benign neglect' towards it.

What is clear however is that, like anyone else not in paid work, an unemployed person trading in a LETS must be actively seeking work, and be available to take up any that is offered. Their eligibility for benefit could well be at risk if they are doing 16 or more hours a week 'remunerative' work, which is defined as work done in expectation of payment. Here two DSS regulations give conflicting guidance: one states that remunerative work includes receiving payment in kind, while another says that payment in kind is not counted as earnings. In 1994 the Secretary of State, Peter Lilley, ruled that, since LETS credits can be exchanged for goods and services in shops and other businesses that participate in a system, a person trading in a LETS should be treated as having an amount of earnings equivalent to their credits.

It is therefore perhaps not surprising that at local level DSS officials interpret the rules in different ways, some treating LETS earnings as money, others as payment in kind. Where it is perceived as the former, LETS groups have argued that this is not valid, because such earnings cannot be used to buy a full range of goods and services, but can only be exchanged for what is available within the local system.

Perhaps the most extreme reaction from the DSS was the demand made on Newbury LETS in its early days, as described by core group member Val Oldaker:

'The local DSS expected our unemployed members to report once a fortnight with details of what they'd earned, worked out by looking at rates advertised in newspapers. This was obviously absurd. If they could earn cash doing those jobs, they wouldn't be working for LETS. One chap who told them he hoped to join our scheme had his benefit stopped immediately – before we'd even accepted him.'

A handful of groups and individuals have had pressure put on them to provide details of their trading. In many cases a clearly-stated description of the aims and purposes of LETS has satisfied the authorities. One LETS member was rather more forthright in his response. He paid a visit to his local DSS office, spelt out his earnings, and asked them what they were going to do about it.

Some groups have used a bit of ingenuity. In Middlesbrough, where members were threatened with potential loss of benefit, they used ticks rather than cheques to represent each transaction.

Elsewhere there has been caution. Drumchapel LETS in Glasgow went to the trouble of getting legal advice from a QC, who concluded that LETS earnings should be counted as payment in kind, since such credits are incapable of being exchanged for any recognised currency. He cited as a legal precedent a case in which money was described as 'that which passes freely from hand to hand in final discharge of debts'.

In Hull a request from the DSS for the names of group members was turned down, and nothing further was heard. Halesworth and District LETS has recently succeeded in convincing the DSS that it need have no interest in LETS trading. Asked in a letter from a local investigator for a list of the names, addresses and services offered by its members, the group's co-ordinator Lucietta Elder declined to send a copy of its directory, which she described as 'a private document belonging to a free association of people, and not the records of a profit-making organisation'.

As part of her response she enclosed an explanatory sheet about LETS, which stated:

'A LETS group is a network of people who agree to provide social favours for each other ... Transactions do not have to be reciprocal between traders. A notional account is kept of the value of each transaction, and this may be stored and spent on services/products offered by anyone else within the group. The notional account is often represented in the form of tokens (eg stones, nuts, etc), and for this reason is unable to be spent outside the LETS group. Because the network is a closed circle the total value of all transactions will equal zero. Thus in themselves transactions cannot be deemed to have any monetary value.'

Thus persuaded the DSS investigator, replying early in 1997, asked her to disregard his original letter, and stated that the Department had no further interest in the matter.

At present advocates of LETS, through the local authorities and LETS Information Exchange, are pressing for fresh guidelines to be formulated by the new Labour government. They also want it to take a more positive view of the role LETS can play in community development and economic regeneration, and in keeping unemployed people in touch with the mainstream labour market by encouraging and enabling them to use their skills.

They certainly seem to order these matters better in other countries. In Ireland there is an informal agreement that LETS earnings do not affect benefit. (See page 84.) The New Zealand government has also been flexible, stating that only income which is regularly received as wages or as part of the receipts of a business is assessable for benefit purposes. In Holland people can now earn up to 3,000 units of local currency without its having an effect on their benefits or income tax.

The most positive government stance is to be found in Australia, where people claiming benefits are now actively encouraged to join LETS systems by the Department of Social Security. A landmark statement in 1993 provided strong official support from the minister, Peter Baldwin, who indicated that LETS credits would not be counted as income for the purpose of the social security income test:

'LETS-type schemes are a useful community initiative which should not be artificially discouraged by social security arrangements. I believe there is a strong case for giving social security clients the flexibility to participate in such schemes. In particular, LETS-type schemes represent a form of activity that assists our clients in keeping in contact with labour market skills and habits, and indeed in contact with the labour market itself.'

The tax issue

The question of how LETS earnings affect a person's tax is a rather more straightforward one. For a start, many people in LETS are either unemployed, or on an income low enough for them not to be liable for any tax. For those who do pay tax, the essential point is that anything they do of a commercial nature within LETS will be liable to tax.

How then is 'commercial' defined? The Inland Revenue makes a distinction between three different types of trade, of which only the first two are liable for tax:

- commercial exchanges, where you are self-employed and offering something connected with your normal business;
- exchanges where you are offering something not connected with your normal business, but which is offered and supplied regularly so as to amount to a business in itself, and is therefore also commercial;
- isolated or fairly infrequent exchanges, where typically you are doing a favour for a friend.

Most LETS transactions count as social favours, and so fall into the last category. If they do not form part of a person's normal trade or business, then they are unlikely to be liable for tax. For example, an accountant would be earning taxable income when doing someone's accounts through LETS, but not if they were providing them with a massage.

In general terms LETS groups have used one or more of the following arguments to show why their activities should not be liable to tax:

- A LETS is a local club where people trade with each other as a hobby or a pastime.

- The activities amount to training and skill-sharing, and until those involved become more proficient, they will not be able to trade in the outside economy.
- A LETS operates on the same lines as a babysitting circle, the credits gained in which are not taxed.
- In relation to goods sold through LETS, if the same sale was made through a car-boot sale or an ad in a paper or magazine no tax would be payable.

The only grey area is if someone gets to the position where they are trading in a LETS in one kind of goods or services on a regular basis, even if this may be a second line of business for them. For example, if a person working as an accountant during the week started to do massage every evening and at weekends on LETS, then the Inland Revenue might become interested in these latter 'earnings'. All will depend on the volume of trading.

Those who run a small business should not overlook another aspect of the need to be open with the Inland Revenue, as one spokeswoman recently observed:

> 'We expect the plumber who as part of his business earns greenlets, trugs, bobbins or whatever, to declare them alongside all his other receipts and profits. Even if he doesn't, a rival will probably do it for him. We've had several cases of firms informing on competitors who are able to undercut prices by operating within a LETS.'

Where it is clear that tax is due, and the LETS unit of exchange is linked to sterling, the Inland Revenue may accept the monetary value of any transaction as the direct sterling equivalent of the local currency. However, they are not bound to do this, and may instead put a sterling value on the income based on 'going rates', which is often called a 'notional value', and which may be quite different from the LETS value of the income. They would of course have to do this anyway if, as is often the case, the LETS unit of exchange has no direct link with the national currency.

LETS themselves, as organisations, are not normally liable for tax, as they are defined as 'not-for-profit associations'. Essentially a LETS involves community development, education and training, and this argument is accepted in principle by the the Inland Revenue. Certainly, Revenue staff who have been canvassed by journalists for an opinion on LETS tend to be fairly relaxed about the idea of local currencies. As one put it: 'We're quite happy about them – members pay tax if they owe it. But I'm afraid we are very old-fashioned. People have to hand over the paper stuff. They can't offer to come round and wash all the windows of Somerset House.'

Clarity on these legal matters is proving especially crucial in some of the newer LETS initiatives being supported by local authorities, as described in the next chapter.

CASE STUDY
BEARA PENINSULA,
REPUBLIC OF IRELAND

Sitting in the spring sunshine outside The Old Bakery café in Castletownbere in West Cork, Jimmy Dowds talks of the impact the LETS idea has had on his attitude to money. 'You start to see how the system is used and manipulated, the way wealth is moved around,' he says. 'It gets you asking questions, talking to people about the world economy, which I had no interest in before. It's a completely different way of thinking.'

Getting involved in a LETS has also prompted him to make a fundamental change in his occupation. Like many of those living on the Beara Peninsula, he has relied for his living on the sea. A fisherman for seven years, his life began to change direction when he became one of the founder members of Beara LETS in 1993. Discovering an interest in computers through compiling the system's directory, he built up a reputation as a computer whizzkid by mending people's machines. Now he is setting up his own computer business.

The remote Beara Peninsula in the South-West of Ireland, stretching out into the Atlantic, may be rough terrain, but it is clearly fertile ground for developing a LETS. It contains a rich mixture of 'blow-ins' – as they call incomers in Ireland – who have come here from other parts of Ireland. Many have arrived from England, including a fair number of self-styled 'refugees from Thatcherism'. Some have come from further afield: a number of retired people from Holland and Germany have bought homes and settled in the area. One professional couple moved from Sweden to Ireland specifically to join a LETS. Having selected Beara as the place to be, they returned home after one winter – because they found the climate too damp.

Many people are involved in the arts and crafts, and there are representatives of most of the world's religions. The Beara LETS members are scattered all round the villages and small towns of this rugged peninsula of rock and gorse, from the tourist centre of Glengariff in the east, to Allihies in the far west, with its vividly painted houses set against a background of scattered disused copper mines. A lot of the paid work is of a seasonal nature, money is tight, and many people have two or three jobs – mostly in agriculture, fishing or tourism – to keep them going. Trading in the LETS is in hags, named after the 'hag of Beara', a famous goddess in Celtic mythology who represents harvest and plenty.

One of the more isolated members is Anne O'Carroll, a legal journalist and language expert, who lives in a simple white one-and-a-half storey house on the wild seashore near the village of Eyeries. Another founder member of Beara LETS, and one of its core group, she runs her home as an English language centre for foreign students, and has used the system to print her publicity material, rent her house out to local groups for weekend stays, and buy the battered 20 year-old red Citroën 2CV that stands outside it. Some days she beachcombs on the nearby shore, rescuing shrimp-pot lids and buoys and trading them with a local fisherman, who in return offers her fresh but slightly damaged fish which can't be sold in the shops:

> 'A lot of people want to join the LETS as soon as they arrive here, because it's a very good way of getting on. The system opens up doors, and people use it a lot. The social thing is also very good: I know just about everyone personally, and it's real contact. It also means that you can do nice things that make you feel like a human being, even if you don't have much ordinary money.'

Beara LETS was the first system in Ireland to have a permanent office. Standing next to the Old Bakery, and built almost entirely for payment in hags, the office – once just a shed – is looked after on a rota basis by four part-time workers, paid through a community employment scheme run by the government's Training and Employment Authority *Foras Aiseanna Saothair* (FAS). Within the office, alongside the system's computer, is a space that serves as the LETS shop, which has its own account in the system. Here people can buy and sell second-hand clothes, household goods, books, toys – indeed anything in reasonable condition that can be stored here and might find a buyer. The shop is the LETS selling-point in place of the stall the group used to run in Castletownbere market once a month. The newest venture is a LETS garden, which is starting up on land just outside the town donated by one of the members. The resulting produce will also be sold in the shop.

In its four-year life Beara LETS has clearly thrived, starting with just three members and building up to around 170 by 1996. Businesses such as the Old Bakery café (boasting 'the last espresso coffee machine before America') and a local hotel have joined. So too has the Beara Arts Society, and this has allowed it to bump up significantly the numbers attending poetry readings and writers' workshops during the local arts festival. A wide range of goods and services is being traded, with food featuring strongly. Some services on offer are unexpected: one member offers to remind people about important anniversaries, another to provide song notation. A few services have been rejected as unsuitable, including the hypnotism offered by one member, and 'casual sex on a regular basis' by another.

But like most other systems, Beara has had problems. At present there is anxiety about the decreasing support for the shop, and the fact that members are tending to buy but not to bring in items to sell. There is also concern about recruiting the necessary labour force for the LETS garden, for which there has been plenty of support in principle, but no actual offers of help. But the most significant problem has been to do with relations with a neighbouring LETS, trading in and around Bantry.

Bantry LETS was originally part of the Beara system. While interest in the idea was growing in Bantry and the nearby towns of Skibbereen and Schull, no one was willing to form a committee and set up a separate system. Since Beara LETS already had an office and a complement of FAS workers – at the beginning there were as many as 11 – it was agreed that they should administer the Bantry accounts. After a year the growing numbers had become difficult to handle, and Bantry finally set up their own system, trading in BATS (Bantry Area Trading System), and soon trebling the number of accounts to 150.

But the split highlighted a certain difference in approach between the membership of the two groups. In Beara there is a fairly relaxed attitude to the running of the system. 'Too much organisation can kill a LETS,' suggests Anne O'Carroll. 'It's much better to have an imperfect system up and running, than a Utopian system that only exists on paper.' In Bantry, with its predominantly middle-class English membership, they admit to being more 'administration-minded'. Similarly, while in Bantry the group has been concerned to involve more local people, in Beara there were some who considered this attitude 'imperialist'.

There were also arguments about an imbalance between the two systems. When the separation finally took place it was calculated that the Bantry members were collectively 2,000 hags in credit, while the Beara accounts showed the same sum in deficit. Subsequently, once inter-trading started, a considerable imbalance built up, caused mainly by Beara members under-spending and over-earning. Finally, after a great deal of debate, not all of it amicable, and with the trading deficit reaching nearly 1,100 units, Bantry decided in spring 1997 to suspend Beara's spending of hags within their system, until the imbalance was substantially reduced. All this led Mike Wilson, a core group member who runs an organic farm near Bantry, to change his mind about inter-trading: 'I used to approve of it, but now I think it's a bad idea,' he says. 'LETS should remain local: we're just encouraging consumerism if people are travelling a long way to buy things they don't want.'

Beara LETS was among the first batch of systems to be set up in Ireland, prompted by a conference on the subject held in Westport, County Mayo, in 1993. This was also the catalyst for groups to be established in Donegal, Shankill in County Dublin, and Westport itself. Since then growth has been patchy and haphazard. Because there is no official national co-ordinating body for the various systems, their precise number is not easy to gauge. But around 30 groups are now thought to be in operation nationwide, trading having spread in the last four years to the counties of Carlow, Clare, Galway, Kerry, Kilkenny, Louth and Sligo.

Despite resistance to it in some areas, the LETS idea has generally become more firmly rooted in Ireland than it has north of the border. According to Tom Simpson, one of the country's early LETS advocates, the impetus has more often than not come from 'blow-ins' rather than from established local people, especially in the West. 'Most people there with any initiative left for America or England years ago, because they felt stifled,' he observes. 'The blow-ins have come with their new ideas and lots of energy, but many of the locals see them as hippie and New Age, and so resent what's happening.'

Where there has been enthusiasm for the idea, it may partly be explained by a tradition of exchanging favours that has existed for many generations in rural areas of the country, especially among farmers. Known as the *meitheal* (Irish for 'working party' or 'band of reapers'), it involves neighbours helping each other out informally with activities such as raising the potato crop or bringing in the hay. Although the practice appears to have largely died out in recent years, as farmers have bought their own machinery and agriculture has become more complex, there are thought to be a few pockets of it left. According to Tom Simpson, the *meitheal* tradition and people's memory of it have played their part in the development of LETS. 'Where you have that kind of tradition and historical link, a LETS will be more acceptable,' he suggests. The link is reflected in the use of the word 'Meitheal' in the names of groups in Cork, Dublin, Tralee, Dingle and Westport.

However, the continuing influence of such mutual aid activities in some areas may also work against the notion of a LETS. Sandra Bruce, who comes from Northern Ireland and was a founder member of the pioneering Stroud system, has been involved in running or studying LETS for seven years. Having recently moved to Donegal, she is in the process of putting together a training scheme and materials to help people set up and run systems in Ireland. She comments:

> 'Where LETS-type activities already exist in the rural areas people look at you as if you are mad. They wonder why you're trying to fix something that isn't broken. There's also the problem of the large black economy, which thrives on secrecy, and so creates a Them and Us feeling. LETS on the other hand offer a different scenario because they depend on openness.'

This liking for informality may mean that even when a LETS has been set up, it remains a very loose arrangement, with little or no accounting taking place. One example of this is the system set up in the town of Donegal, which after four years still has only around 25 members. There is no committee or proper administration; people are writing out cheques, but the accounts are not being added up; and yet members continue to trade. As Tom Simpson observes: 'In the UK you have accounts, calculators and computers; in Ireland it's much more informal, it's something you keep in your head.' Nevertheless, groups with membership of more than 100, such as those in East Clare, Dublin, Galway, Shankill and Westport, tend to use a computer for their accounting and directories.

Another important reason for the relatively enthusiastic response to LETS in Ireland lies in the supportive attitude of the Irish government, one that stands in marked contrast to that in the UK. This enables unemployed people to join LETS without any worry that they might lose their benefits by doing so. Richard Douthwaite, who set up Westport LETS and who has been an influential voice in the LETS movement in Ireland, explains in his book *Short Circuit* how this came about:

> 'The Department of Social Welfare accepted arguments by Westport LETS on behalf of all the Irish systems that it was in the public interest that the

unemployed be free to take part, because this would keep their skills alive, maintain their work habits and, since informal networks are so valuable to job-hunters, raise their chances of hearing about national-currency-paid jobs. Participation was also likely to maintain their health, we said – because many studies had shown the damaging effect unemployment has on the health of those experiencing it and their families – and therefore to save the state resources it might otherwise have to spend on medical, psychiatric and social care.'

In August 1993, the government indicated its acceptance by replying that it would not withhold benefits as long as LETS did not 'begin to encroach on regular taxed and insured employment'.

The involvement of workers through the FAS community employment scheme, as in the case of Beara LETS, has also provided a good impetus for some of the Irish systems. But this kind of official involvement has been seen by some groups as a two-edged sword. Members of Bantry LETS, for instance, had strong views on the matter, as Mike Wilson recalls:

'We had six workers for a year, they ran the market stall, and their help and energy were very useful. But in the end we decided we would be better off without them. We felt as if we were becoming part of the state bureaucracy, and it also meant that members were expecting things to be done for them. Now that we've made the decision, there's more goodwill, more community feeling.'

Though some people believe that LETS in Ireland might benefit from having an umbrella organisation to provide advice and information for individual groups – as the LetsLink bodies do in England and Scotland – there seems to be no immediate chance of one being set up. Meanwhile Sandra Bruce, who is involved with the LETS in Donegal, is pushing ahead with her efforts to help the movement to grow. In addition to running a training scheme, she hopes to be able to get leaflets about LETS to all unemployed people in Ireland, and to take the idea into schools, working in partnership with people already active at the grass roots. Although her work is still at an early stage, she has been encouraged by the positive response she's been getting:

'The idea of LETS is about timing as much as anything else. I have a strong feeling that this is the right time for it to make progress in Ireland, with the loss of community and social networks, rising unemployment, and people feeling under so much pressure. Every conversation I've had with agencies and government departments is pointing in the same direction: people instinctively respond well to the idea.'

She's convinced that in five to 10 years' time LETS will become an established fact of life in Ireland:

'I believe that the Irish people will adopt LETS in a way that no other country will or can. In the end they're people who won't sell out for money, people for whom community is a bloody important word. What happens here could be a beacon for other countries.'

Certainly developments in Ireland are beginning to attract the attention of other countries. Beara LETS was recently visited by an official from the Belgian Ministry of Finance, as part of a fact-finding mission for a political study group which aims to assist with the growth of LETS in Belgium. After a day on the peninsula he was particularly impressed with the presence of FAS workers, as evidence of the supportive policy of the Irish government towards the development of LETS.

HELP
FROM
OUTSIDE

8. HELP FROM OUTSIDE

'If you think it will lead to people paying their council tax in LETS, then you're living on another planet' – council officer

As LETS have become more established and spread into many different areas, so there has been a steadily growing interest in them by local authorities. As high unemployment persists and local services continue to suffer cutbacks, many councils are starting to see LETS as a valuable element in their economic development, Local Agenda 21 or anti-poverty strategies. A few, operating in some of the most disadvantaged communities in the UK, have even begun to act as catalysts in getting groups off the ground.

But the response to outside help has been mixed. Some people believe LETS should be self-sufficient, or that they should grow organically from the bottom upwards at their natural pace. Others are simply deeply suspicious of or hostile to anything initiated or supported by their council. Such views are well understood by many council representatives: at a recent meeting of officials involved with LETS in many parts of the country, it was acknowledged that council support, despite its potential benefits, could threaten the autonomy of LETS, disempower people who belong to them, and produce an over-reliance on funding which may turn out to be only short-term.

Nevertheless, by the spring of 1997 it was estimated that 25% of LETS in the UK were receiving help of some kind from their local authority. Nearly half of the rest were either seeking it, or said they would welcome it; one-sixth had yet to make up their mind on the question; and only 6% were against.[1] The fast-developing council interest was reflected in the formation in 1996 of a national Local Authorities and LETS Information Exchange, which now has over 50 councils on its database. A recent analysis it carried out of the different types of support being given to LETS showed that groups were being helped in Bracknell, Bristol, Cardiff, Derby, Devon, Glasgow, Gloucester, Hereford, Leicester, Nottingham, Oxford, Powys, Reading, Redditch, Somerset, Stroud, Wakefield, and in six London boroughs.

In many cases the support has been relatively modest: providing groups with equipment, offering them help with publicity and meeting rooms, giving access to internal mail systems or assisting with the printing of posters and leaflets. In some areas existing or potential LETS groups have been offered modest start-up grants. In a few the council has gone a step further and actually joined a LETS. Calderdale was the first to do so. Instead of giving a grant, the council provided £500 worth of services to members, which could be paid for in the local currency, favours, but which would be accounted for in the council's accounts. It allowed LETS members to use council facilities for photocopying, mailing and printing, and the council could then use its credits to top up grants to local charitable organisations. More recently, the town council in Frome joined the LETS as a trader, supplying photocopying, hire of the market hall and the use of sports and play facilities for 100% fromes, in return for gardening and decorating. And in Exmouth the LETS group rented office space from the council for cockles, in exchange for supplying various services.

Some groups have resisted council involvement. Derby LETS recently declined assistance from its city council. Nithsdale LETS in Scotland, after discussing plans for Dumfries and Galloway council to join and for a region-wide currency to be created, backed away from the idea, concerned at the possible restrictions that might be placed on the group's activities. 'We'd been going about a year, we were a fairly friendly group of some 65 members, and were really very lax,' says co-ordinator Sarah Dearden. 'Suddenly it seemed to us that we were getting into big-time economics. So we decided to pull out.'

Manchester, now the biggest LETS in the UK with 700 members, was at one stage discussing £10,000 worth of support from the city council, which was enthusiastic about the idea. The core group suggested that instead of being classed as a grant, the sum should be converted into a loan, to be paid back over several years in the local currency, bobbins. But in the end the plan foundered on the group's uncertainty about whether it would be able to raise sufficient bobbins.

The strongest support has come from the handful of authorities that have appointed full-time LETS development officers. Hounslow was the first to do so, in 1994. (See case study, page 29.) More recently Bradford, Greenwich, Redditch and Shepway have followed suit, while in Liverpool the council has set up a three-person LETS Development Team as part of its Local Agenda 21 initiative.

The work being carried out in large inner-city estates in some of these areas is beginning to bear fruit. In Bradford, which already has a city-wide LETS with 265 members, new groups were set up in spring 1997 on some of the most impoverished estates, funding coming jointly from Europe and the council. In Liverpool a new LETS has just been established in Walton, joining three groups already operating in the south of the city. In Greenwich, one of three boroughs already covered by the 250-strong Thamesdown LETS, a group is about to start up on a classic run-down working-class estates in the inner city.

The development officers in these three areas all admit they have had difficulty overcoming barriers. Chief among these has been the deeply engrained suspicions felt by people towards the council. Tariq Shabbeer, Bradford's LETS development officer, pinpoints the problem: 'It's to do with being perceived as the man in the suit and tie,' he says. 'As soon as you mention the words "council" or "European funding", they just turn off.' Jan Hurst in Greenwich has encountered similar difficulties: 'When a council is making cuts in some department, you're just seen as part of it. So overcoming distrust and cynicism is very difficult. It's hard to convince people that the LETS will not be council-run.'

The situation is aggravated in Liverpool because of the long history of conflict between the city council and community groups. 'It means that you're bound to get a negative response at first,' says Mike Maguire, manager of the LETS team. 'But when you explain and talk it through, most people accept that you're not wanting to run the group, and that it's not just the council's latest wheeze.' In Bradford they have found that the best way of overcoming this problem is to ensure that any explanations about LETS are given by local people presenting the scheme to their neighbours, with the council acting simply as a catalyst.

People on these estates have also been worried about the effect any LETS trading might have on their entitlement to benefits. 'This has proved a massive barrier, a huge fear,' Mike Maguire says. 'What with that worry, and the Jobseeker's Allowance, and then the "snoopers' hotline", they were very suspicious.' A similar fear existed in Bradford. 'The biggest worry was that the bailiff was going to come round and take everything back that they had traded,' Tariq Shabbeer says. In Greenwich such fears proved to be well founded, when staff at the Woolwich DSS office announced that people would need to inform them before they started trading in a LETS. 'I must admit I was horrified by this restriction,' Jan Hurst says.

90

In Liverpool, one of the poorest parts of Europe, the focus for LETS has been on the high-rise estates where, unusually, 60% of residents are over 60, and around 20% are disabled. Many people in these two categories felt they would be unable to cope with trading in a LETS because of their age or condition. Mike Maguire highlights the issue:

'We've tried to challenge these stereotypes. There's a tendency, especially among working-class women, to undervalue things they have done in the past. We've tried to turn that on its head, and show them the things they do, such as making clothes or reading to their grandchildren, are very useful. The potential is great, but it takes a while for it to sink in. When it does come through people are quite excited, and respond warmly to the idea.'

But not everyone reacts in this way. In Bradford efforts to get a LETS going in the Little Horton area proved unsuccessful – and yet a group was soon afterwards established in the neighbouring Canterbury Estate. Tariq Shabbeer recalls:

'Only two people were interested in Little Horton. The rest either didn't want to get involved, or said they still didn't understand the idea. It's hard to know what makes the difference, but it just seems to come down to who the individuals concerned are.'

Experience has shown that a core of enthusiasts is essential in order to get a LETS off the ground. But such people may be hard to find in places such as the Ferrier Estate in Greenwich. Jan Hurst observes:

'A lot of people there say they love the idea of a LETS, but don't want to get involved in a steering group. There's also a lot of competition for people's time: many of them are busy doing other things on the estate. People are also shy at first, although they become more interested when they see their neighbour becoming involved. You definitely need to get some LETS champions on board.'

Like others starting in a LETS, people on these estates have found it hard to grapple with the idea that you can go into debt without incurring any charges or penalties. 'If everyone starts with a zero balance, it's only the most committed people who spend,' Tariq Shabbeer argues. His solution with the new groups in Bradford has been to credit all members with 50 units of local currency to start them off.

Another anxiety has been personal safety. People on the Ferrier Estate, for instance, were concerned enough to suggest that members should carry identity cards, complete with photo. For the benefit of people trading with others they have never met, each transaction would carry a job number known only to the two parties concerned, and available from the co-ordinator's database. Similar fears evidently exist in Bradford, where a community officer said of one of the estates: 'What's most in demand is having someone sit in your house to stop it being burgled when you're out.'

While the involvement of local authorities has real pitfalls and drawbacks, there's no doubt that such support has helped to launch many innovatory schemes, some of which are described in the next chapter.

CASE STUDY
RURAL COUNTY: SUFFOLK

S ally Moxon is not sure how she would have survived without the Gipping Valley LETS. 'Even though I live way below the poverty line, I've been able to sustain myself in ways that I never would have otherwise,' she says. 'It's like finding an oasis in the desert.'

Not long ago she was running her own company in Harrow, earning £350 a week providing advice and computer training to small businesses. Then her business folded. Now she lives alone on income support in a bare flat on the edge of the Suffolk town of Stowmarket, surrounded by half a dozen cats.

'Belonging to LETS helps you rise above the poverty line and regain some self-esteem,' she explains, over coffee and Guinness cake. 'I have no transport, but I've been able to get lifts. I only had one pair of sandals, but I was able to get some boots last winter. The system has enabled me to get food, not to mention clothes which I wouldn't normally have been able to afford.' In exchange, she offers computer training and advice about setting up a business to other members of the group, which trades in talents. Thus sustained, she has started to find a new life, and is now studying for an Open University degree.

LETS has begun to catch on fast in Suffolk. Six years ago there was only one group trading, in Bury St Edmunds; now there are 12, operating also in Beccles, Eye and Diss, Framlingham, Gipping Valley, Hadleigh, Halesworth, Ipswich, Lowestoft, Stonham and Stowmarket, Sudbury and Woodbridge. In addition, groups in the Aldeburgh and Leiston area and Felixstowe are considering setting up a system.

And now a further step has been taken. Suffolk InterLETS was established in 1996, initially to enable the groups to exchange information and advice. But it soon led to inter-trading between groups, and now a county-wide directory, LETS Pages, has been launched. It is a development that has divided opinion within some groups, and one (Framlingham LETS) has declined even to take part for the moment. Enthusiasm for inter-trading is strongest among group co-ordinators and the more active members. One of these is Simon Raven, a prime mover in establishing Suffolk InterLETS:

> 'There's quite a lot of angst about inter-trading. Many people think the whole joy of LETS is that it's local, and that you shouldn't go outside to trade. Others believe there are benefits, since you can get a wider range of things if you trade with other groups, and it makes sense in relation to the county-wide anti-poverty campaign.'

As in other predominantly rural areas, trading in and around the pretty towns and villages of Suffolk has helped to break down isolation, especially among those new to the county. 'I think the famous Suffolk reserve is only on the surface, but in today's world people can be very insular,' says Janet Hamilton, co-ordinator of Woodbridge and District LETS, which now has over 100 members. 'There are some shy ones, people who are unsure of themselves or rather overwhelmed by life. With LETS they suddenly find there are things they can do, and life becomes a little easier.'

Some of the goods and services on offer to Woodbridge members, who trade in flints, reflect the nature of the area. They include coppicing, shelter for passing walkers, old timber doors, exercising ponies, a fruit press, beekeeping equipment, and tuition in charcoal burning, as well as the usual mixture of alternative therapies and house repairs. Among the 'wants' are boat repairs, fresh goat's milk, horse manure delivery, land on which to keep a pig, sheep feeding, and lifts to market.

Most of the Suffolk groups hold regular social events, to encourage people to trade and exchange ideas. Gipping Valley LETS has recently gone in for 'themed' evenings focusing on clothes, plants and crafts, and is considering holding evenings devoted to alternative therapies and skill demonstrations. Such events often result in people discovering new possibilities.

Childcare is a staple element of trading in many groups, enabling hard-pressed parents to benefit. Sarah Matthews, a mother of three small children, is co-ordinator of Ipswich LETS, which has about 60 members, and trades in quays. 'It's a terribly useful system for having children looked after,' she says. 'People say, "Oh, it's only childcare", but that's very important. Normally you feel you can only ask people once or twice, but that doesn't have to apply with a LETS.'

Group activities are also becoming a feature in some groups, with decorating and house-moving gangs proving popular. But some involve a more regular and challenging collaboration. A Woodbridge couple recently offered their large garden for use as a 'community garden' by LETS members. Besides growing food, the plan is to maintain wildlife habitats and create new ones, and grow new flowers and herbs. The dozen members involved have regular community gardening days, charging flints for the time they put in, and getting them back when the produce is sold. Such a variation on the normal one-to-one trading can bring its own difficulties, since even like-minded people have their differences. Janet Hamilton observes: 'There's the ardent rotavators and flame-gun-brandishing lot, and the permaculture people, who don't want to disturb a single butterfly. Although it's all very amicable, the ideas are not immediately compatible. I think we're going to need two gardens.'

Such initiatives are important where food is seen as a key element of LETS activity. Although Suffolk is perceived as a relatively wealthy county, it has pockets of high unemployment and plenty of examples of poverty. As Sarah Matthews points out: 'You can't feed your kids on benefits alone.' So Suffolk InterLETS has become involved with the county's anti-poverty campaign, and has started to look at possibilities such as setting up food co-operatives – one dealing in organic produce is just getting off the ground in Woodbridge; establishing a Suffolk credit union with local collection points; and working with mental health user groups. Recently it has had a £1,000 grant from the council, which has been distributed among all the groups to help with basic items such as photocopying.

Despite growing links, the Suffolk groups opt for different approaches. Some are tightly organised, are keen to ensure a reasonable trading balance, and keep firm control on levels of trading. Stonham and Stowmarket LETS, for example, closes the account of anyone not trading for six months. Others are more laid-back in their attitude. 'Some people trade, some don't,' says Janet Hamilton. 'It's important they don't feel pressurised.'

Some groups deliberately avoid taking what they describe as a 'monetarist' approach. One such is Halesworth and District LETS in East Suffolk, which trades in LETS. Simon Raven, a former teacher who was instrumental in getting the group going, lives in an eighteenth-century terraced house on the outskirts of the village of Wenhaston. Talking in his small office crammed with LETS paperwork, he suggests the group is breaking the normal rules:

'People get into LETS currency, and it's fun to play with it, but it's still money. We soon abandoned the notion of zero-sum accounting, because we found it was of no consequence. So we just give new members 10 LETS, to allow them to put a toe in the water and get things going. By doing that we're asking what LETS are – the answer being something that we can pluck out of thin air! Our current position of being 2,250 LETS down would horrify a conventional accountant. But it's a confidence-building exercise. Eventually we want to do without audits, to reach such a sense of belonging to a community that it will be more like an extended family, with no tally required. Some people have already got to that stage.'

The Halesworth group is, as he puts it, 'left, liberal and alternative', but as in other groups people are keen to broaden the base of the predominantly middle-class membership. They are keen to draw in more people such as Mandy Birch, a single mother with twins aged 10, who lives in a small council estate on the edge of the seaside town of Southwold. Sitting in the front room of her council house, on a sofa newly upholstered as a result of a LETS transaction, she talks of what she has gained from her involvement in the group:

'The benefits for me are more to do with friendship than anything else. It's good for a single mother like me to be able to go to meetings. You can take your children along and you don't feel you're intruding. It's helped me realise that, even though I'm on the social, I've got a voice in a small way. I've made new friends, I've been to yoga, to circle dancing, to a picking day on a farm. I'm actually a bit scared of just phoning people up, but going to the meetings means you can get to know them first.'

Although she doesn't trade as much as she would like to, she has had an oak tree planted in her garden, had her car mended, and tried alternative therapy for her children. In exchange she's sold painted glass items, offered second-hand clothes, and helped people move house. 'I'm in debit most of the time, but it doesn't matter,' she says. 'It doesn't get you down, it proves you're using the system. And it all helps you to live with people.'

Many of the Suffolk groups were started by a hard core of people wanting to improve the well-being and welfare of their community. Some of the co-ordinators and pioneers believe that considerable progress has been made on this score in a relatively short time. 'People feel they have more control over what they're doing, instead of relying on the government or council,' Janet Hamilton says. 'There's been a re-awakening of values that have been forgotten.' Sarah Matthews agrees: 'Some people see it as part of the revolution. I don't know about that, but I certainly believe it's changing the way people think, and getting them to revalue what they can do.' Sally Moxon also believes there have been great gains: 'The more you hear about what people can do, the more ideas you get, and the more people can realise their potential.'

BRANCHING OUT

9. BRANCHING OUT

'All I think we are doing is lighting little candles, but that is better than cursing the darkness' – Peter North, LETS writer and researcher

A s the network of LETS has grown, so their potential for expansion into new areas of life is being explored more thoroughly. Innovatory schemes have shown how a LETS can be used to enhance some of the most basic aspects of people's lives, such as food, health, housing and education. Other developments include the setting-up of credit unions, the appearance of women's groups, plans for an arts LETS, and the growing involvement of voluntary organisations.

Food

For many involved with LETS, food is seen as one of the keys to the growth and development of the idea. They believe the present climate could be a propitious one. People are now exploring ways of producing healthier and more varied food locally, looking for alternatives to the domination of the supermarkets, with their high proportion of processed goods, many imported from thousands of miles away. The growing interest in organic produce, in food co-operatives, and new small-scale forms of food distribution ties in with the LETS approach, which has its roots in the local community. Initiatives are now being co-ordinated under the banner of a LETS Eat! project.

Many groups, notably in the West Country, are starting to use gardens and allotments to enable more food to circulate within LETS. In Plymouth, where many of the 120 members have small gardens, they have been growing produce both at home and in two allotments rented by the system from the city council. Any surplus has been traded for plums (the currency, not the fruit) with other members. Bristol, Brixton, Leamington Spa and Stroud are other places where allotments have been exploited within the system. In Gloucester a double allotment is being used by some 30 LETS members. 'An allotment scheme can help to broaden the appeal of LETS,' says John Rhodes, one of the LETS Eat! co-ordinators. 'Getting more food into the system increases its value because it's meeting a basic need. It also helps to increase trading, which in turn can bring in new members, both rich and poor.'

LETS are also linking up with food co-operatives. In Telford, Shropshire, distributors for a local Green Growers co-operative come into town with bags of seasonal organic vegetables, which can be paid for in wrekins, the local currency. Growers in Bideford, Chard and Malvern are also now willing to trade in LETS currencies, as are the organisers of box schemes in places such as Bristol, Leicester and Stourbridge.

One of the more developed schemes is in Stirling in Scotland, with 120 members. The LETS food co-operative has a delivery service and a team of packers, all paid in the local currency, groats, which are funded through a subscription levied on members. The co-operative buys in organic bread and cakes, and pays a driver in groats to pick up organic vegetables from Fife. Mark Ruskell, a development worker for LetsLink Scotland, says:

'The Stirling system is small, but the food co-operative has helped to develop the system by increasing turnover, enabling members to meet, and providing a regular monthly event on the system. Most of all, it's given them an ethical, cheap and environmentally responsible range of products.'

Mental health

People with mental health problems come from all walks of life, but are often unable to use their skills in the mainstream economy. A LETS allows them to do so as and when they choose. This way of thinking lay behind the pioneering project Positive Mental Health LETS, set up in 1995 in Warminster, Wiltshire. The idea was for mental health service workers and users to exchange skills and services through the region's well-established Tradelink LETS, which by then had 350 members. People experiencing mental, psychological and stress-related problems could gain access to therapies, counselling and other services which they either could not get on the National Health Service, or could not afford.

The project was run in conjunction with the Bath Mental Health Care Trust, Warminster Social Services and the local mental health team, and was based in the town's Beckford Community Centre. Here psychiatric nurses, massage practitioners and acupuncturists were available to offer regular treatment, for which the users paid in the local currency, links. In return they offered goods or services of their own: another aim of the project being to enable people to take part in ordinary life by focusing on their abilities rather than their disabilities. 'People with mental health problems are not usually good at developing or maintaining friendships, and so they become isolated,' says Gina Smith, co-ordinator at the centre. 'Developing supportive networks in this way can help to prevent mental illness.'

During its first 18 months the project was used by around 50 people, and appeared to attract a much broader cross-section of people than most LETS. According to the scheme's originator, Harry Turner, it provided at least £60,000 worth of complementary health care and associated support. 'With a LETS such as this one, you have a feeling of power, of being in control,' he suggests. 'It's not the same relationship as you have with the National Health Service.'

This too is the sentiment at the LETS Make it Better project in Stirling, set up through the charitable Mental Health Foundation, and linked to Stirling LETS. Launched in spring 1997, and operating in the same building as the Stirling LETS office paid for by the council, it already has 80 members, many of them referred to the project by GPs, consultants, community psychiatric nurses, and social services. There is a weekly drop-in lunch, at which the participants decide on what trading events to hold, and then organise them. 'What they say they like is the reciprocal nature of the relationships they have through trading, and the chance to work with members of Stirling LETS in larger-scale building and decorating projects,' says development worker Lesley Rowan. 'And the project has become much broader because of the very positive response it has had from the professionals and the statutory bodies.'

The good take-up has been echoed by that at the Creative Living Centre in Manchester, which has 145 members after being in existence for little more than a year (see case study, page 107). Indeed, the LETS and Mental Health idea has been spreading rapidly: as many as 25 groups now have such schemes, in places as diverse as Brent, Guildford, Hampshire, Middlesbrough, North Solihull, Oxford and Redruth. In Surrey the Runnymede social services has started a LETS in the local hospital in Chertsey. Other groups, in Glasgow, Suffolk and York, are contemplating establishing similar arrangements in conjunction with local mental health bodies.

Housing

Interest in LETS is growing among housing co-operatives, some of which are now having a proportion of their building work done in exchange for local currency. In Manchester trading has been set up by a housing association, allowing people to pay a percentage of their rent in bobbins in exchange for giving their labour. Meanwhile in Islington the council is supporting a LETS Build pilot scheme, while in Brixton the LETS is exploring the possibility of building some housing itself, on land set aside for community use.

Education

Several independent schools have joined a LETS, either just to help their finances or to assist less well-off parents in paying fees. Leading the way have been the Steiner schools, which already have a tradition of letting families on low incomes pay part of their fees by working in the school.

Others to have joined a system include a nursery school in Surrey, which offers a similar arrangement to members of Godalming LETS. The Bath Small School, started by parents, belongs to the city's LETS, and uses the system to hire out the building for olivers. In Wiltshire many of the parents who set up The Orchard School in Bradford-on-Avon in 1991 were already members of West Wiltshire LETS, and the principle that the £35-a-week fees could be paid partly in the local currency was built in from the start. The school had an unusually high proportion of families on benefits, so the possibility of paying around 25% of the fees in links made a significant difference to several parents. But the scheme eventually ran into difficulties. 'We were trying all the time to strike a balance,' says Daniel Johnson, one of the founders. 'But there were a lot of overheads, and in the end the school couldn't afford to carry on with the arrangement.'

A few state schools are also getting involved, usually for financial or community reasons – or both. Longdean Comprehensive in Hemel Hempstead, Hertfordshire, has already joined the local group. The staff use the system as a way of making contact with the local community. Recently they brought in a professional painter and decorator to supervise students painting a classroom. In return the LETS group has been given the use of a room for meetings. Other schools, such as Sir Wilfred Martineau, a large inner-city comprehensive in Birmingham, are seriously considering joining their local groups.

There is also some interest in LETS within adult education. One of the community colleges in North Yorkshire has had to restrict the number of its non-vocational evening classes, since the low levels of funding and high number of concessionary students mean they cannot afford to run them. As a way of making more courses available, the college is exploring with Richmond and District LETS the idea of joining the system, and collecting course fees and paying tutors in the local currency.

Credit unions

There are many similarities between credit unions and LETS. Both are schemes run by members of a community for their mutual benefit; they share a common philosophy, that by working together people can achieve more than they do individually; and both can be of particular use to people who are unemployed or living on a low income. However, in other respects they are different: while credit unions have strict rules, LETS tend to be more flexible, adaptable and idiosyncratic.

Nevertheless, several LETS groups are looking at the possibility of establishing a credit union for their members, on the basis that they already have the 'common bond' that is a condition of setting one up. One group prompted to explore this idea is the county-wide Suffolk LETS, where three people have recently been arrested on suspicion of charging exorbitant interest rates on illegal loan deals. But the first group likely to get one going is Manchester LETS, which has a steering group in place and a lot of enthusiasm for the idea. 'There's more administration involved than in a LETS, so we're being a bit cautious,' says Siobhan Harpur. 'But there's so many people wanting to join and so much interest, I feel it's very likely to happen soon.'

Women's groups

While women tend to join LETS in greater numbers than men, and very often dominate the core group, groups confined to women only are rare.

Quines LETS in Glasgow seems to be the sole group of this kind in Scotland. (See page 56.) In England the only known group is Naari LETS in Leicester, which is being set up to try to lessen the isolation of Asian women.

Smita Shah, the city's economic development officer, has been involved in setting up the group:

> 'Asian women tend to be marginalised and confined to their homes, where traditionally hosiery has been the only outwork available. We hope LETS trading will encourage them to do other things, such as teaching Asian cookery or Gujerati, perhaps outside the home.'

The group already exists on an informal basis as Naari LETS (*naari* is Hindi for woman), with a membership of 120 whose unit of exchange is the *moti* (Hindi for a pearl, once a token of barter in India). However at present little trading is taking place, so the council has offered the group a small grant to produce a directory. Smita Shah says:

> 'We're giving them a fair bit of hand-holding and awareness-raising. We're trying to get people to say what they want, what they can offer, and then see what's missing. Then the council might be able to provide specialist training courses where there's a demand. For instance, if a lot of women wanted to learn knitting, such a course would be free to members, and the tutor would be paid in the local currency.'

It is hoped that eventually it may be possible to create some small-scale enterprises that will allow the women to practise these kinds of skills in a neighbourhood centre. One step in this direction was made recently with the first inter-trading event with Leicester LETS, at which services and produce were exchanged.

The arts

Many artists and craftspeople belong to a LETS, notably in those groups which have a strong 'alternative' flavour to their membership. At present Les Moore of LETSGo is planning to set up a national Arts LETS, which would be open to anyone working in the arts. So far, in the London area, he knows of 50 interested people.

Voluntary organisations

The involvement of voluntary organisations in LETS has taken several different forms. At its simplest, it involves an organisation joining a local group, as the Woodcraft Folk has done with Ealing LETS, allowing members to join by paying in emus. In other places they have been drawn in to more specialist schemes: several local branches of the mental health body MIND, for example, have been involved in discussions about setting up LETS and mental health schemes.

One of the more ambitious initiatives is LETSWork, an innovative scheme established in Bristol in 1996, linking up 15 community groups and voluntary organisations such as Community Service Volunteers and the National Federation of City Farms. The idea is for the bodies to trade with each other in services such as training, organising events, leaflet design, and the hiring out of rooms and equipment. The members can also trade with the seven other LETS in and around the city. However, trading so far has been minimal, according to the scheme's co-ordinator Ben Barker. 'Organisations seem to find it hard to get into the act with LETS,' he says. 'But at the moment it's too early to say whether the idea will succeed.'

Developments like these underline the potential of LETS to inform many different areas of people's lives. But their impact is likely to remain restricted unless certain hurdles can be overcome. These are dealt with in the final chapter.

CASE STUDY
INNER-CITY SUBURBS
MANCHESTER

S ix years ago Rose Snow's world was turned upside down when the death of a close friend so shattered and disturbed her that she spent six weeks in a mental hospital. Though going there had been her own idea, she didn't like the place, decided to leave – but was compelled to stay after being 'sectioned':

> 'Up to then I had had a successful professional and personal life.
> Afterwards I lost everything – my career, my marriage, my friends. I was
> very angry, because I felt I was the victim of an arbitrary decision which
> had ignored my life as a creative, competent person, and which had forced
> a new identity of madness upon me.'

It was this anger that eventually prompted her to set up the LETS Make It Better (LMIB) project in Manchester in 1995. Its aim was to enable people with or recovering from mental health problems to use LETS as a tool to help one another, to make user-friendly alternative therapies easily accessible to them, and to break down the social isolation experienced by many who suffer this kind of distress. It was inspired partly by the pioneering work being done in this field at the Beckford Community Centre in Warminster (see page 99), and partly by her own experience as a member of the well-established Manchester LETS. 'I was living in a new area and was very isolated,' she recalls. 'I'd said goodbye to my friends and my marriage, I was very poor, and physically ill. LETS not only gave me economic spending power and an outlet for my intellectual needs, it also gave me a new family.'

Now recovered from her traumatic experience, she talks in the front room of her house in South Manchester of the struggle she has had to get her grass-roots project onto a firm footing. A lot of development work has been done: she has set up an advisory group, met with mental health user/survivor groups around Manchester, and collected case-studies of individuals who have benefited from an involvement with a LETS. She was also involved in 1996 in organising and staging the second national conference on LETS and Mental Health, at which speakers told of the challenges that mental health problems can pose, and the ways in which LETS are helping people to overcome them. And for two years running she has been rewarded with a commendation in the regional Health Challenge Awards for the project's commitment to improving the health of the region.

However, though it has support from the local health authority, the social services department and a voluntary action agency, she has not yet got the financial backing for LMIB that she now desperately needs. As a result, she has continued to run the project single-handed from her home. Though her front room is relatively uncluttered today, it is usually swamped by LETS files and documents. 'The project seems to be taking over my life, and quite honestly I sometimes feel like just giving up,' she admits.

For the moment though she is pressing on. One of her principal aims is to get a LETS up and running on the Wythenshawe Estate in South Manchester – she is now on the steering group for a proposed community forum there. The second largest estate in Europe, Wythenshawe has, she says, many acute mental health problems:

> 'I don't mean people are psychotic, but there's a terrible amount of family stress. There are young mothers there who don't have anybody to turn to, who are going up the wall, getting close to breakdown, threatening suicide. What we would hope to do is help them to build a caring community. We would offer a support system through the LETS, so they could get help from other people with things like cleaning and looking after their kids, and gain access to a variety of alternative therapies. Ultimately we'd like to open a holistic health centre on the estate.'

Despite the uphill struggle, her work has already produced some concrete results elsewhere in the city. The contacts with user/survivor groups has led some individuals to join Manchester LETS, which now boasts 700 members. Others have set up new groups within Greater Manchester: LETS and mental health schemes of one kind or another are now up and running in Stockport, while another is about to be established in Trafford. A similar scheme also operates in nearby Macclesfield.

Sally Miller, a former waitress, is a member of the small but growing Stockport LETS, set up by the local social services department in conjunction with Stockport MIND. So too is her daughter Stephanie, who is recovering from a nervous breakdown. As the two of them sit in the back kitchen of co-ordinator Felicity Glass' house, the group's meeting place, Sally speaks warmly of the support the group has given both her and her daughter:

> 'We've been made to feel wanted. When you have a breakdown you lose a

lot of friends, but this is a wonderful way of meeting people who care and understand. There's very little help in the community, and what there is is not very useful. We've made many new friends through the group. It helps you to feel wanted rather than being on the scrap heap.'

The group is not formally called a mental health LETS, because it is felt that such labelling is best avoided. But as it happens, the majority of its 14 members have had some contact with the mental health services. Most work part-time or are unemployed; as a group they come from a mixture of backgrounds. As Felicity Glass says:

'Mental health is no respecter of class. We've attracted a real cross-section of people with all manner of talents and experiences. Some are living on low incomes, some are very well educated. But we've kept it simple. Instead of sitting down and swopping ideologies, we just invited people along. We don't ask them to delve into their personal history.'

The group meets formally once a month, and trading takes place at a very practical level. 'It's a way of helping yourself and helping other people at the same time,' Sally Miller says. 'You don't have to be academic, you can just do things like gardening and babysitting. It makes you realise that you have more to offer than you think.'

Although the group is still in its infancy, it already appears to be helping some of its members to regain a degree of confidence in themselves. Felicity Glass, who is funded by Stockport council as a community resource worker, has noticed the difference. 'People already seem to be getting benefits from belonging,' she suggests. 'We have heated debates, and people are gradually becoming more vocal and more confident. In the end of course it's all about human beings.'

Such a philosophy also underlies the mental health scheme in Prestwich in the north of Manchester. The Creative Living Centre (CLC) is a holistic project providing a range of activities and services for 'people who have experience of emotional distress'. Established in 1996 to offer mental health users and survivors 'a unique supportive place to come and be yourself', it is backed by the Mental Health Services of Salford NHS Trust, which has provided the premises and funding for a development worker, Siobhan Harpur.

'It's fundamental to the project's philosophy that people are approached as individuals with a mind, body and spirit,' she says. 'Another essential ingredient is that people are able to define their own needs and make their own informed choices as part of a process of taking responsibility for themselves.'

A key element in this self-help approach is the new Creative Living LETS, which after being in operation for little more than a year already has 145 members. Regular LETS markets are held at the centre, when stalls are set up, food is shared, and people can put faces to the names they have seen in the directory and trade in the local currency, links. At other times LETS members can tap into complementary therapies, and workshops on topics such as communication, prejudice reduction, and careers support. Auctions have also been held, with relaxation, shiatsu and haircuts being among the items under the hammer. Members can also get involved in helping with the centre's latest venture, a horticultural garden which is being created to add to the healing atmosphere of the place.

Once the centre is properly established – it is about to become a charity – the aim is to help groups in other towns in the area such as Bury, Salford and Oldham. In the last a group is already using the CLC's administration: they have an insert in the CLC directory, which allows people to trade locally, but also to make use of the centre's more specialist services, such as relaxation, group hug therapy, or Bible and spiritual readings.

Siobhan Harpur underlines the system's value:

> 'A LETS fits comfortably into the holistic philosophy of the centre because it can have a real impact on our sense of well-being and self-worth. It also provides an opportunity to integrate the community so that we're all working with and for each other's support. We encourage each other to look at our strengths, not to focus on illness or any other factor which may hold us back from realising our full potential. And trading in a LETS means we can begin to overcome some of the vulnerability and loneliness that people who have mental health problems and emotional distress so often know every day.'[1]

THE
WAY
AHEAD

10

10. THE WAY AHEAD

'If we are ever to achieve independence in our lives and communities, the right to issue our own currencies is one of the issues over which we must expect to have a fight' – Richard Douthwaite, *Short Circuit*

The LETS movement has reached an interesting but critical stage. With nearly 450 groups established in the UK and Northern Ireland, most of them since 1990, there is enough experience around for it to have become clear what the main barriers are to further development. If LETS are to grow and thrive into the next century, several issues need to be addressed.

Undoubtedly the most critical one concerns the UK government's attitude to the benefits question. If LETS are to have any real and lasting impact on the poorest and most disadvantaged sections of our society, then people who are unemployed or on low incomes will need to be totally confident that they can join and trade in a system without any danger of their benefits being lost. At present they cannot do so, because judgment on these matters is left in the hands of officials in local Department of Social Security offices, and is therefore arbitrary, inconsistent and confusing.

On this matter the UK government is a long way behind those of other countries such as Australia, New Zealand and Ireland, which take a much more positive and relaxed attitude to LETS, seeing them as valuable community initiatives worthy of support, and making that position abundantly clear. The UK government, by way of contrast, can offer only 'benign neglect'.

What is needed from the new Labour government is some positive action to clear the LETS idea of any suggestion that it is part of the black economy, or that people's income could be affected if they join a system. One obvious way forward is being proposed by the Local Authorities and LETS Information Exchange, which has suggested that the government could amend the regulations relating to the Social Security Contributions and Benefits Act, and exempt the trading activities of LETS members from its definitions of work. LETS payments would then be treated neither as income nor as earnings derived from employment. Under a proposed new definition of LETS, a system would be approved if the government was satisfied on three counts: that it was a local community-based system, that its primary concern was to help people maintain their labour skills and keep in touch with the job market, and that it was not a system run for profit. The advantage of such a change to regulations is that, in contrast to the introduction of new legislation, it could be effected in a relatively short time, perhaps as little as six months.

Another obvious need is for the collective wisdom that has been gained in the last few years to be made more accessible to members of existing and potential groups, to save them from re-inventing the wheel. In this matter the LetsLink umbrella bodies in England and Scotland have been valuable sources of advice and information, but are necessarily limited in what they can do given their minimal human and financial resources. But while many LETS co-ordinators and core group members have been not only dedicated but extremely effective in carrying out their unpaid tasks, there is no doubt that some systems have suffered from a lack of experience in key areas. While many people would not want to lose the informal, friendly ethos that characterises so much LETS activity, a little training in certain key skills could go a long way to improving the effectiveness of LETS. Local authorities are just beginning to get interested in the training issue, and should by now have a pool of experienced tutors to draw on for any courses they might decide to set up.

It is clear that the involvement of local authorities in support for LETS is set to increase, possibly dramatically in some impoverished areas. But there is a widespread feeling that this will be effective in the long term only if it involves discreet support, rather than heavy-handed 'top-down' imposition of the idea on a community. A LETS is essentially a personal system which allows individuals to determine more of their own lives, and anything that tends to diminish that element should be resisted.

Some people believe that LETS can function in the mainstream economy only if they attract many more members and begin to draw in a significant number of businesses. Those organisations such as LETS Solutions and LETSgo which are trying to pilot schemes to involve small businesses are at present only able to scratch the surface, mainly through lack of funds. If businesses are to be persuaded of the value to them of a LETS, their interest needs to be carefully nurtured. So this kind of sustained development work needs to be properly supported, perhaps with a mixture of private- and public-sector funding.

It is often said that a LETS can have a positive effect on a local economy, but there is little significant evidence to show the scale of the impact. Now that LETS have a track record, the moment would seem to be ripe for a pilot scheme to be set up, in order to try and identify that effect. Such a scheme has recently been launched by the Department of Commerce and Trade in Australia, and the results are keenly awaited. The project aims to increase the economic turnover of a depressed small town in Western Australia by 10% in a year, using LETS trading. So far half the 36 businesses have signed up, and the aim is to involve half the 800 households by the end of 1997. A similar government or local authority initiative in the UK or Ireland, perhaps in two contrasting areas, one rural and one urban, could provide welcome evidence of the real economic value of LETS, as well as of their relatively low cost in relation to community regeneration.

Will LETS survive into the next century, or will they peter out as many other community-based initiatives have done? Certainly they have already brought significant benefits to thousands of people in the UK and Ireland. But they have still touched only a tiny proportion of the population, and have yet to make a real impact on all but a few of the poorest and most disadvantaged members of our society. There are also those who criticise LETS for creating an alternative economy which simply serves to further exclude those involved from the mainstream economy.

Yet the essence of LETS fits in with the very concept of sustainability which is increasingly seen to be vital to the future of the planet. It encourages people to act locally while thinking globally, a notion which is likely to be as relevant to the survival of communities in the next century as it has been in the present one.

LOCAL CURRENCY NAMES: A SELECTION

ENGLAND

Avalon, Glastonbury *Gebo*
Bath *Oliver*
Bradford *Brad*
Brighton *Bright*
Bristol *Thanks/Favours*
Calderdale *Favour*
Canterbury *Tale*
Carlisle *Reiver*
Castle *Onny*
Cheltenham *Current*
Clevedon *Doofer*
Dartmoor, North-East *Tin*
Derby *Wadeva*
Devon, North *Talent*
Diss, Norfolk *Disc*
Dorchester *Mart*
Exeter *Exe*
Exmouth *Cockle*
Falmouth *Plum*
Forest of Dean *Vicar*
Frome *Frome*
Gipping Valley *Talent*
Godalming *Watt*
Halesworth *LETS*
Hampshire, South-East *Hamlet*
Ilkley *Wharf*
Ipswich *Quay*
King's Lynn and West Norfolk *Shell*
Lancaster *Lune*
Leicester *Leaf*
Leicester *Naari Moti*
Lewes *Trug*
Malvern *Beacon*
Manchester *Bobbin*
Medway *Medlet*
Newbury *Newberry*
Newcastle *Nut*
Newquay *Net*
Norwich *Loke*

Oxford *Boxlets*
Plymouth *Plum*
Reading *Ready*
St Austell *Starlet*
St Leonards *Gem*
Salisbury *Ebble*
Scunthorpe *Pig*
Sheffield *Stone*
Somerset, South *Brock*
Southampton *Solent*
Stoke *Stoke*
Stonham and Stowmarket
    Stone/Pebble
Stroud *Stroud*
Stubbington *Badger*
Swindon *Don*
Telford *Wrekin*
Totnes *Acorn*
Warwick and Leamington *Oak*
Wellington, Somerset *Tone*
Wiltshire, West *Link*
Woodbridge *Flint*
York *Yorky*

London

North *Pledge*
South-East *Sec*

Barnes *Pond*
Brixton *Brick*
Camden *Lock*
Croydon *Croy*
Ealing *Emu*
Hackney *Favour*
Hampton *Tag*
Harrow *Harmony*
Hillingdon *Hillingdon Pound*
Hounslow *Crane*
Kingston *Beak*
Lewisham *Fule*
Merton *Eco*

Newham *Hammer*
Portobello *Bello*
Southwark *Peck*
Sutton *Sutt*
Thameside *Anchor*
Tower Hamlets *Hamlet*
Waltham Forest *Beam*
West Hampstead *Ecu*

WALES

Cardiff, Adamstown *Orbit*
Cardiff, St Mellons *Tab*
Carmarthen *Merlin*
Clwyd, Vale of *Ddraig*
Haverfordwest *LETS*
Lampeter *Lamp*
Penarth *Pebble*
Powys, South *Beacon*
Rhondda *Cymoedd*
Taf and Teifi *Teifi*
Wrexham *LETS*

SCOTLAND

Arran *Rowan*
Bute *Bute*
Campsie *Campsie*
East Lothian *Ellet*
Edinburgh *Reekie*
Findhorn *Buzz*
Glasgow Drumchapel *Drum*
Glasgow Kelvingrove *Kelvin*
Glasgow West *Groat*
Moray Firth *Nessie*
Nithsdale *Doonie*
Quine *Quine*

Shetland *Tern*
Skye *Skye*
Stewarty *Queenie*
Stirling *Groat*
Tweed *Tweed*

NORTHERN IRELAND

Banbridge *Link*
Belfast *Pint*
Coleraine/Portrush/Portstewart
    Gheeghan
Crumlin *Crumb*
Derry *Acorn*

REPUBLIC OF IRELAND

Beara *Hag*
Carlow *LETS*
Clare, East *Grainne*
Clontarf *Acorn*
Cork City *Cuid*
Dingle *Taisce*
Donegal *Sods*
Dublin, Food Co-op *Luach*
Dublin, South City *Grain*
Dun Laoghaire *Dun*
Dundalk *Eco*
Galway *Luach*
Gort *Coole*
Inishowen *Wheen*
Kells *Sceilig*
Shankill *Skill*
Sligo *Gill*
Tralee *Ready*
Westport *Reek*

NOTES

For full publishing details of books and reports referred to in these notes, see Further Reading (page 116).

Where no source is given, the material comes from interviews or correspondence with the author, or material supplied by LETS groups.

1 HISTORY

1 Margaret Cole, *Robert Owen of New Lanark*, 1953; F Hall and W P Watkins, *Cooperation*, 1937.
2 Cole, *op. cit.*
3 David J Weston, 'Local Currencies', briefing paper, New Economics Foundation, 1991.
4 Olive and Jan Grubiak, *The Guernsey Experiment*, 1960.
5 Harold Sculthorpe, 'LETS', and Colin Ward, 'Learning about LETS', *Raven* 31, autumn 1995; Richard Douthwaite, *Short Circuit*, 1996.
6 Philip Blake, 'The Chain of Good Neighbours', *Reader's Digest*, October 1979.

3 NUTS AND BOLTS

1 LetsLink national survey, 1996.

5 THE PROBLEMS

1 Colin C Williams, 'The Emergence of Local Currencies', *Town and Country Planning*, December 1995.
2 Hugh Deynem, Kate Ormrod, and Debbie Paynter, *LETS in Cornwall*, 1995.
3 Helen Barnes, Peter North and Perry Walker, *LETS on Low Income*, 1996.
4 Nic Evans, 'A Proposal for Inter-LETS Trading', Totnes LETS, May 1994.

8 HELP FROM OUTSIDE

1 LetsLink national survey, 1996.

FURTHER READING

BOOKS

Victor Anderson, *Alternative Economic Indicators*, Routledge, 1991.

Margaret Cole, *Robert Owen of New Lanark*, Batchworth Press, 1953.

Guy Dauncey, *After the Crash: The Emergence of the Rainbow Economy*, 2nd edition, Green Print, 1996.

Ross Dobson, *Bringing the Economy Home from the Market*, Black Rose Books (Canada), 1994.

Richard Douthwaite, *Short Circuit: Strengthening Local Economies in an Unstable World*, Green Books/Lilliput Press, 1996.

F Hall and W P Watkins, *Cooperation*, Cooperative Union, 1937.

Peter Lang, *LETS Work: Rebuilding the Local Economy*, Grover Books, 1994.

ESSAYS

Richard Douthwaite, 'Local Currency', *Resurgence,* no. 131, November/December 1987.

Olive and Jan Grubiak, 'The Guernsey Experiment', pamphlet, Omni Publications, California, 1960.

Peter North, 'LETS and Communes', in *The Cooperative Guide to Living*, Diggers and Dreamers Publications, 1995.

Harold Sculthorpe, 'LETS: Local Exchange and Trading Schemes', *Raven*, no. 31, 1995.

Colin Ward, 'Learning about LETS', *Raven*, no. 31, 1995.

David J Weston, 'De-Linking Green Pounds from the Big System', *New Economics*, 1991.

RESEARCH

Helen Barnes, Peter North, and Perry Walker, *LETS on Low Income*, New Economics Foundation, 1996.

Hugh Deynem, Kate Ormrod, and Debbie Paynter, *LETS in Cornwall*, Cornwall LETS Forum, 1995.

G J Seyfang, *The Local Exchange Trading System: Political Economy and Social Audit*, MSc thesis, University of East Anglia, 1994.

Colin C Williams, 'Local Purchasing Schemes and Rural Development: An Evaluation of Local Exchange and Trading Systems', *Journal of Rural Studies*, 1995.

Colin C Williams, 'Local Exchange and Trading Systems: A New Source of Work and Credit for the Unemployed?' *Environment and Planning*, vol. 28, 1966.

Colin C Williams, 'The New Barter Economy: An Appraisal of Local Exchange and Trading Systems', *Journal of Public Policy*, vol. 16, 1966.

LETS ORGANISATIONS

UNITED KINGDOM

LETS Connect
12 Leasowe Green
Lightmoor
Telford TF4 3QX
Tel: 01952 590687
Fax: 01952 591771

LETS Solutions
124 Northmoor Road
Manchester M12 5RS
Tel: 0161 224 0749
Fax: 0161 257 3686
and
7 Park Street
Worcester WR5 1AA
Tel/fax: 01905 352848

LETSgo
23 New Mount Street
Manchester M4 4DE
Tel: 0161 953 4115
Fax: 0161 953 4116

LetsLink Northern Ireland
20 Beechwood
Banbridge
County Down BT32 3YL
Tel: 018206 23834

LetsLink Scotland
31 Banavie Road
Glasgow G11 5AW
Tel: 0141 339 3064

LetsLink UK
61 Woodcock Road
Warminster
Wiltshire BA12 9DH
Tel/fax: 01985 217871

IRELAND

Irish LetsLink
Lower Aiden Street
Kiltimagh
County Mayo
Tel: 00353 94 81637
Fax: 00353 94 81708

INDEX